Skull Orchard Revisited

Art, Words & Music by Jon Langford

with David Langford
Photographs by Denis Langford

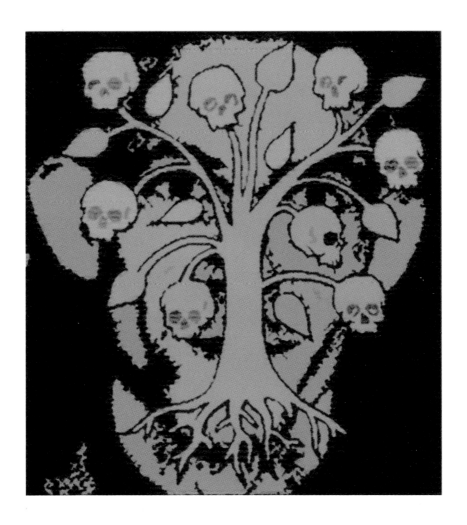

Verse Chorus Press   Portland 🍃 London 🍃 Melbourne

For Kit and Den

Jon Langford and the Burlington Welsh Male Chorus would like to thank Warren & Chris Hellman and Dawn Holliday

Published by Verse Chorus Press, PO Box 14806, Portland OR 97293. info@versechorus.com

Distributed to the trade in North America by Publishers Group West (pgw.com), in Europe by Turnaround (turnaround-uk.com), and in Australia by Dennis Jones & Associates (dennisjones.com.au)

Back cover photograph by Bryan McBurney
Design: Steve Connell
Color guy: Scott Nasburg

Printed in China by C&C Offset Printing Co., Ltd.
CD manufactured in China.

ISBN: 978-1-891241-30-7

Library of Congress Control Number: 2010942660

FIRST EDITION

INTRODUCTION

An ugly, lovely town (or so it was and is to me) . . .

    This sea town was my world; outside a strange Wales, coal-pitted, mountained, river-run, full, so far as I know, of choirs and football teams and sheep . . . , moved about its business which was none of mine.
                                    – Dylan Thomas, *Reminiscences of Childhood*

I was born on the border, and we talked about 'the English' who were not us, and also 'the Welsh' who were not us.
                                                        – Raymond Williams

The songs on *Skull Orchard* are mostly about Newport, the ugly, lovely town I was born in, and the not so strange Wales beyond. My mum was from the valleys and my dad was from the 'Port. Like Raymond Williams, he thought of himself as neither English nor Welsh, but on that point he and my mother would never agree. Her family was full of miners, rugby players, pigeon fanciers – there was even the odd Welsh speaker. I moved up to Leeds in 1976 (the year they closed most of Llanwern steelworks) and then to Chicago in 1992, but the eyes of an exile can't help looking back, and I can't help going back there.

    Newport is full of ghosts for me now, and sometimes when I walk the streets of the town centre I feel like a ghost myself – lost, gone, unrecognizable . . . an invisible man. My dad used to take me and my brother Dave down to the docks on Saturday mornings to see the big Soviet cargo ships and the squat little tugboats. You can't even get in there now, though there'd be precious little to see if you did. Outside the dock gates, where the Transporter Bridge straddles the brown, tidal Usk, lies Pillgwenlly (or Pill, for short). Like Tiger Bay in Cardiff, people came there from almost everywhere on earth, and anything a lonely sailor might need was always close at hand. As teenagers we were drawn there, to the pubs that turned a blind eye, crazy hot curries, the jazz club, the folk club, and smoky after-hours joints where Joe Strummer, for one, heard reggae music for the first time. Johnny Sicolo, a former ship's cook who ran the legendary punk-rock club TJ's, was from Pill. His dad got off a boat from the Seychelles and forgot to get back on.

Like most seaport towns, Newport's eyes were fixed on the horizon. There was so much leaving and so much arriving. Even the accent isn't strictly Welsh – there's a hard, urban *a* and a bit of Bristol in there somewhere, which is true of my family as well. Once I sat with my Uncle Bob as he traced our family tree back to 'some posh bloke from England who used to come round every six months.' So there we were, culturally muddled and racially impure, with class divisions apparent even at the tea-table. During the miner's strike my dad, a Ted Heath Tory, would have to grit his teeth as my grandmother screamed 'Scab!' out of the back window of his Volvo at the passing coal trucks.

I was born the same week the Sputnik went up, in a maternity hospital in Caerleon, an ancient Roman settlement with a ruined bathhouse, sunken amphitheater, and loads of pubs (one of which was formerly run by Anthony Hopkins' parents). We lived up the Gaer, and from our junior school we could see the docks and the Channel and the weird-colored smoke and flames escaping from the petrochemical plants at Avonmouth. Our playground was an ancient British fort, where my dad once sat in a hole in the ground with a single mortar shell waiting for the Germans to come. At night his mother would crawl through the bracken to bring him a flask of tea.

From just about anywhere in Newport you can see Twmbarlwm, a round green mountain with an unlikely nipple on top. This Silurian burial mound inspired Arthur Machen's novel Hill of Dreams, but beyond it, invisible to us, lay the blighted industrial valleys of South Wales, where the road from Bryn Mawr to Bleanavon ran like a scar through a moonscape. In 1966, when I'd just turned ten, a torrent of mine waste smashed into the village school in Aberfan, killing 116 school children. It was man-made disaster, fuelled by cynicism and neglect, that hung over our childhoods like the Bomb. We drove by there the following summer on our way to the coast and saw all the little crosses up on the hillside.

A few years ago, completely out of the blue, Sassy Hicks (ex-bassist of Carlton B. Morgan and the Supernormals) called and asked me to contribute a painting to raise money for the Garndiffaith Rugby Club's history committee, which was putting together a book about the club and involving disaffected local youth in the process. Garndiffaith is a tiny mining village high on the hills above Pontypool, a valley town where sizeable chunks of my family still live. Wild, drunk Chartists marched on Newport from up there back in 1839 (the last bloody workers' uprising); after the miners' strike of 1984-85, Blaensychan Colliery was shut down and the Garn was crippled. At one point they didn't even have a rugby team . . .

> There were problems in the community with homes and shops being broken into, also vehicles being stolen and burnt out . . . This had a drastic effect on the Social Club, as people were afraid to leave their homes at night and the bar trade was dropping drastically.
>
> – Maldwyn Cooper, *A Look Back in Time*

I did them a painting of an anonymous rugby player in Garndiffaith RFC kit and went up to meet them at the Club with my eldest boy Jimmy and cousins Mark and Freddie. We watch the Garn thrash Senghenydd and gazed across the valley at a vast rocky outcrop known as the Devil's

Heap of Stones. You can see it all from up here, right down the East Valley, fifteen miles to Newport and the sea.

After the game, we went to the concert room and bar (rebuilt by volunteers after an arson attack in the 1990s) where author Mal, Brian, and the boys laid out their history of the South Wales valleys – the story of the Senghenydd miners who were buried with their final pay packets after the country's worst pit explosion, a US plane that crashed up by the Devil's Heap of Stones one night during the war, the time Gareth Edwards' Cardiff side came up to play the Garn in 1977 ('We was robbed"), and the players' wives and girlfriends who got organized and raised the money to buy the Lasgarn View ground, which boasts a pitch that is perhaps (but maybe not) the highest in Wales. Beer and laughter, tall tales and undeniable truths, were mixing freely that night.

We tried to sell the painting through the web site of Yard Dog, my gallery in Austin, but nobody was biting, so we organized a benefit gig in a Cardiff

boozer; the Garn boys came down on a bus with their wives. It was a great night and we managed to raise a few quid for the book project.

When *A Look Back in Time* finally came out, I bought a few copies for friends and family to make up for the painting not selling. It's an exhaustive, funny, and candid history of the club and the community it's so central to. On page thirteen I found a team photo from 1938 or 1939 showing my mother's long-dead cousin Gordon Rosser, unsmiling and arms folded, second from the left at the back, and his brother Sid, who lived out his days in the Garn, just below him in the third row.

I came back to this *Skull Orchard* record like I come back to South Wales – out of a concern and connection to place, and a feeling there's still something to find and something to talk about. Raymond Williams and Arthur Machen were haunted by the border lands of Southeast Wales long after they left them, while across the planet dark, toxic visions of 1970s Leeds (my other old haunt) discomforted novelist David Peace throughout his exile in Tokyo. In *Low Life*, an amazing book about New York City, Luc Sante explores time and place on Manhattan Island and pinpoints physical locations where history seems programmed to repeat itself and millions of eerie threads stretch back down the years.

> THE BELIEVER: I love the scene near the end of *Low Life* when you look up at a shard of sky on the Lower East Side that you imagine someone might have glimpsed one hundred years ago. I do that all the time in New York City and feel a weird connection to everyone who's ever lived here. Something ghostly connects people to the city and its history, don't you think?
> LUC SANTE: I think that's true of all cities. Since I wrote *Low Life*, I've read Iain Sinclair on London and Louis Chevalier on Paris and I know that those kinds of occult bonds exist in spades in those places, especially since they're much older.
> – *The Believer*, 2004

In 2007 we played a benefit show in another seaport town. It was for a charity and social project called Sweet Home New Orleans, which has been attempting, with some success, to rebuild the broken jigsaw of the city's fragile post-Katrina music scene. Organizer Jordan Hirsch talked to me about the same importance of place, those same occult bonds. Their whole plan was dependent on knowing exactly who lived where and interacted with whom on which street corners and hot spots across the city, where the ghosts walk, and who's still carrying the torch.

In South Wales Margaret Thatcher organized and executed her own natural disaster, an ironic coda to Aberfan: the mines are gone, the unions smashed, tips grassed over, a way of living lost forever, deliberately obliterated. You can sign on the dole or flip burgers. So who holds what's left together? In New Orleans it was always the social clubs; in a battered Welsh mining village, of course, it's the rugby club. Raise your glasses to the history committee of Garndiffaith RFC! At least someone's doing something with care and patience and dignity. Let the record state: I have a lot of time for old Welshmen in rugby-club ties . . .

. . . And down by the muddy sea in the 'Port, Johnny Sicolo is gone and the pubs are shutting down for good, the chains have the town centre in a death grip, and the youth is revolting, throwing up and pissing on the ground where Chartist rioters bled and died for the vote. But they still haven't torn down the Transporter Bridge – in fact, the dangling gondola that once carried workers from Pill to the steelworks is moving again, protected by a dragon called Hysbryd O Ddur, the Spirit of Steel. The jobs are gone, too, but the ghosts still ride back and forth, suspended by wires over a murky brown river flowing backwards beneath them, up and down, round and round. And the last time I walked back up from Pill to the Lahore Restaurant (after loud, weird music and cans of Strongbow in a renovated chapel), the back streets were creepily silent yet lovely; the cracked pavement shone wet with rain under the blurry orange streetlights. I still can't ever wait to get back.

TOM JONES LEVITATION

Where ever you wander
Where ever you'll be
Up there in the Rhondda
Down here by the sea
We're calling you home,
    calling you home
And this time it's to stay

And I, I can fly
Over the clouds and over the rain
And I can see the greedy hand
Of the vandals who ravaged the
    land

It's just waiting to happen
The equation's the same
And the rules are as dirty
Though everything's changed
I see it all, you're still so small
And disasters will take new
    names

And I, I can fly
Over the valleys and over the
    hills
And I see the secrets
The kisses and quiet
I see the moonlight in the valley
It's taking me back
Where the earth is still black
And the murderer lies under
    your feet
Taking me back . . .

A SOUTH WALES ALPHABET
by David Langford

A. . . . One of the Langford traditions was to drive for miles and miles in order to walk up Rudry Mountain in Glamorgan (it's called Rudry Mountain, though Rudry Modest Hill or Rudry Quite Large Tump would be more accurate names for it). There were **ADDERS** there, actually allowed to roam the wild without a BBC film crew to record every wiggle and hiss.

My confrontation with a Rudry adder is a cherished family legend, many times retold at the watering-holes where aunts gather. At the time, I was young enough to be in the habit of carrying a large plastic sword and scabbard wherever I went. It was a sunny day, and they found me carefully keeping the coiled snake in my shadow because (according to hazy memories of something I'd read in the *Children's Encyclopedia*) this was suppose to stop it getting overexcited. My plan was to lure this reptile into the scabbard – which was just about the right size – and carry it triumphantly to Cardiff Zoo. Instead it slid off into the bracken.

Unlike many of our family legends, this one is entirely true. But I never quite believed the uncle or cousin who knew for a fact that we'd all been in deadly danger, because [*voice drops to a low, blood-curdling tone*] a friend of a friend had seen just such an adder uncoil like a spring and *leap thirty feet* to fix its fangs in the doomed victim.

Though I never managed to import adders into the household, we did once find a slow-worm at the far end of Burnfort Road from our old pebbledashed house there. 'It's not a snake,' I learnedly explained, 'it's a legless lizard.' We then discovered how to tell the sex of a slow-worm: if it promptly gives birth to a litter of jelly beans, it's a she. The jelly beans twitched feebly. Dad performed Caesarian operations with a razor blade, releasing tiny silver snakelets with black stripes down their backs. They were almost unnervingly cute.

We kept the family in an old fishtank and fed them gourmet slugs, but maybe the wrong kind of slugs since the mother quietly died in there. The surviving little ones staged a mass escape while being exercised on the back lawn, and vanished into the rockery. For all I know, whoever now lives in the Burnfort Road house is still wondering what idiot established a breeding colony of snakes in the garden. Don't worry! They're only legless lizards.

B. . . ■ It is not true that my experiments with home-made explosives left Newport High School an insurance write-off that wasn't worth repairing. Not long after I left, though, the school moved from its St Custard's redbrick building near the railway station to a dull new home in **BETTWS**, well outside town on the Cwmbran road. I was moved to commit blatant plagiarism of John Betjeman:

> *The High School's transplantation*
> *In nineteen seventy-two*
> *Has left for contemplation*
> *A rather dismal view.*
> *On masonry and woodwork,*
> *The concrete dust collects:*
> *Sing praises to the good work*
> *Of female architects!*

Our old headmaster D. Parry Michael followed his school to Bettws, and I went to see him there on some now forgotten errand. He kept me waiting in his outer office while he and other visitors – including that female architect – sang the whole hymn for my benefit. Of course I deafly couldn't hear a word through the closed door, but it gave me a warm glow when DPM told me afterwards.

> *Within that grey emporium,*
> *Who knows what madness lurks?*
> *How like a crematorium,*
> *How like a sausage-works!*
> *How high the phallic tower*
> *Thrusts upward through the air,*
> *To symbolize the power*
> *Of teachers everywhere!*

A touch of poetic licence there, since the 'tower' was hardly more than a tall narrow chimney. The word before that tended to get mumbled when sung on official headmasterly occasions, like one of those bits of the National Anthem that no one quite remembers.

> *O concrete grey and dismal:*
> *Behold the wondrous sight!*
> *O corridors abysmal,*
> *O gay fluorescent light!*
> *Sing on, with hymns uproarious –*
> *From rain and storm aloof –*
> *Look up! and oh how glorious,*
> *It's leaking through the roof . . .*

...on's whole secondary school career happened at Bettws. He reported bitterly that the older staff from Newport High had somehow acquired a deep suspicion of pupils called Langford and tended to blame them for just about any unsolved crime. I couldn't possibly comment.

COMING DOWN: Demolition of the old Bettws High School, Newport
CB_1581

End of an era as old school is demolished

THIS is what remains of the old Bettws High School as it is slowly reduced to a pile of rubble.

Contractors from the Cuddy Group stepped in to demolish the buildings that are no longer needed following the construction of the £25 million Newport High School.

With the sports hall and swimming pool already among the ruins, work continues to remove the remaining infrastructure, a project that is set to be completed by mid-March.

Aeron Thomas, senior project manager for Leadbitter, the company that built the new school, said that a team of 16 people is employed to crush and sort the building materials, of which most will be put to use elsewhere. "The majority of the building materials will be recycled, with the crushed concrete probably being used in the foundations of new buildings.

"Some of the old school's white goods were sent to Uganda to support the local children there," he said.

As reported by the Argus in October 2008, cupboards, desks and chairs were sent to Kisis Primary School in Buranburye, Eastern Uganda, to help with their education.

The land is to be sold by the council to make way for a new housing development in the near future.

P.S. Early in 2010, yielding to everyone's opinion of its architectural value, the decrepit, weather-stained and horrible Bettws school was demolished. To us it seemed hardly any time since it was shiny, new and horrible.

14

Inside the Whale

We saw a better world just around the corner
Time's arrow pointing down some happy trails
Big, clear dreams arising over the event horizon
But no light escapes
From inside the whale
Long blue summer nights, some basic human rights
The lunar landing craft, a donkey's ear and tail
All swallowed up as midnight struck
It's so dark down here
Inside the whale
An end to hunger, equality, under the sea
Inside the whale
Progress, progress, rose tinted glasses
cock-eyed optimism all cracked and paled
And all the astronauts and the Kennedys got caught
Down in the depths
Inside the whale
So naive, this white boy's dream
Tucked up in bed
Inside the whale

DOLPHIN INFORMATION AGE

It was the dolphin who told me about the old sea captain and all the fuss you people made. I have to say it didn't ring any bells at all. Dolphins are really smart, smarter than you could ever imagine. This one had read the book from cover to cover and when she finally bumped into me – literally: she collided with my scarred white flank somewhere off the west coast of Africa! – she could scarcely believe it. She never even saw me (so much for that mighty dolphin sonar).

She said you'd been looking for me forever. How was I supposed to know? 'You're most famous,' she clicked. 'You're bloody mythic,' she added with a frantic nodding screech. Apparently, I discovered, I am the very rarest stuff of legend. This dolphin knew everything. She even knew my name, which at that time was, of course, still unknown to me. Dolphins don't have names; they're way beyond all that. So we'll just call her Flipper.

THE FIRST RETURN TO THE DEEP

Like me, she ditched dry land hundreds of generations ago. The time was right. All that earthly tattle and crap was weighing her down, the gravity of it all depressed her. With every hailstone and pecan nut that fell and cracked her rapidly expanded mammalian skull she inched deeper into the wetlands, before finally shedding her fur and feet to slip back beneath the waves forever. Too much responsibility. It was the only intelligent thing to do. Who has the will to stay grounded when right next door the neighbors are frolicking in the pool?

But even as she soared through the warm bright bubbly blue, Flipper still nursed a hankering for that old abandoned world of dust and roots and shale. She was endlessly curious

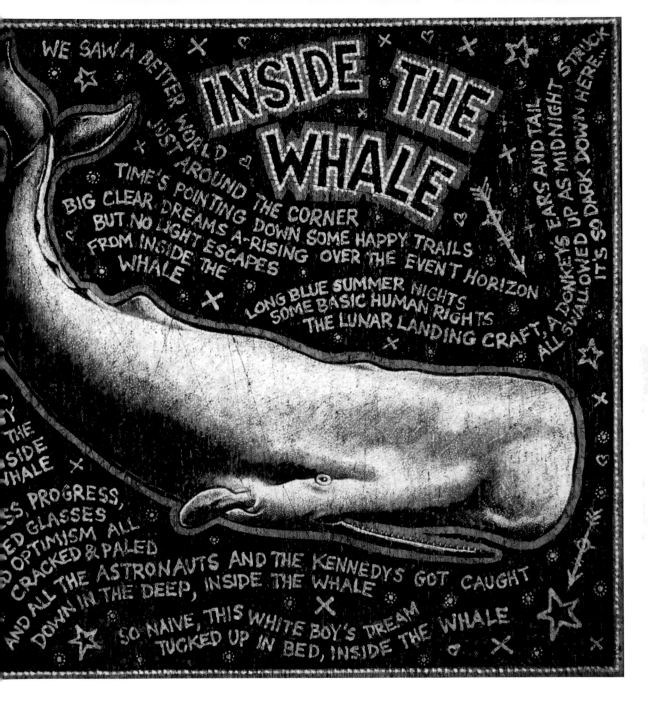

INSIDE THE WHALE

WE SAW A BETTER WORLD
JUST AROUND THE CORNER
TIME'S POINTING DOWN SOME HAPPY TRAILS
BIG CLEAR DREAMS A-RISING OVER THE EVENT HORIZON
BUT NO LIGHT ESCAPES
FROM INSIDE THE
WHALE

A DONKEY'S EARS AND TAIL
AS MIDNIGHT STRUCK
ALL SWALLOWED UP
IT'S SO DARK DOWN HERE...

LONG BLUE SUMMER NIGHTS
SOME BASIC HUMAN RIGHTS
THE LUNAR LANDING CRAFT, A DONKEY'S

THE
SIDE
WHALE

SS, PROGRESS,
ED GLASSES
OPTIMISM ALL
CRACKED & PALED
AND ALL THE ASTRONAUTS AND THE KENNEDYS GOT CAUGHT
DOWN IN THE DEEP, INSIDE THE WHALE

SO NAIVE, THIS WHITE BOY'S DREAM
TUCKED UP IN BED, INSIDE THE WHALE

17

and could never resist exposing her smooth grey beak to the dry air above and taking a peek at what you lot were up to. A dangerous game indeed, for – as she told me – there are waves in the air which are pretty much the same as the waves in the sea, except that a terrible monster has clogged them all up with his pictures and numbers, his bleeps, lies and messages of doom. That's probably why Flipper's sonar went haywire and I'm washed up on this mud bank.

CRAP BOOK REVIEW NO. 1

This is an ill-compounded mixture of romance and matter-of-fact. The idea of a connected and collected story has obviously visited and abandoned its writer again and again in the course of composition. The style of his tale is in places disfigured by mad (rather than bad) English; and its catastrophe is hastily, weakly, and obscurely managed . . . The result is, at all events, a most provoking book – neither so utterly extravagant as to be entirely comfortable, nor so instructively complete as to take place among documents on the subject of the Great Fish, his capabilities, his home and his capture. Our author must be henceforth numbered in the company of the incorrigibles who occasionally tantalize us with indications of genius, while they constantly summon us to endure monstrosities, carelessnesses, and other such harassing manifestations of bad taste as daring or disordered ingenuity can devise . . . We have little more to say in reprobation or in recommendation of this absurd book . . . Mr. Melville has to thank only himself if his horrors and his heroics are flung

The capital city, 12 miles away to the west, full of sin and spectacle and evocative district names like Splott! Our mother's greatest dread about her boys was centred on **CARDIFF**. She lay awake at nights worrying that one or other of us would be contaminated by sordid big-city influence and (shudder, shudder) *pick up a Cardiff accent.*

Victoria Park in Canton, Cardiff used to have a tiny zoo that was famous for Billy the Seal. Billy had been accidentally caught in the net of a fishing-boat somewhere off the Irish coast in 1912. He wallowed happily in the zoo for many years, with one brief outing when Canton flooded in 1927 and Billy went exploring: he was found trying to board a tram in Cowbridge Road. When Billy died in 1939 it turned out that there had been a basic error and that he was, in fact, a she. The zoo is long closed but there's still a statue in the park of its star attraction Billy the Seal – which shows how rare exciting events used to be in Cardiff.

Sadly, the dates are all wrong for my pet theory that Billy helped inspire Arthur Machen's 1895 horror story 'The Novel of the Black Seal".

C...

D...

Our father's name – as we've spent all too many years explaining – is spelt **DENIS**, not Dennis. By an uncanny coincidence this is also Jon's middle name. Likewise, Dad's brother was Geoffrey and there was an Uncle Claude in the family. My wife Hazel spotted the trend when she added all these alien forenames to her laboriously researched family tree. 'Your father's lot aren't Welsh at all!' she hissed. 'You're all *Normans*!"

In the long run, everyone really comes from somewhere else.

Mr. Dennis George Langford, of Newport, and Miss Catherine Pearse, of Croesyceiliog, after their wedding at St. Woolos.

E...

At secondary school I was vaguely aiming for a career in science (which eventually turned out to be a five-year stint in a squalid hut at the Atomic Weapons Research Establishment). A budding scientist must carry out world-shaking **EXPERIMENTS**, and so – generally in collaboration with my schoolmate Chris Faulkner, who was less responsible than me – I did my best to push back the frontiers of knowledge. Gobbling up vast quantities of detective novels and science fiction was also helpful. Some important discoveries:

• The formula for traditional black gunpowder given in H. Beam Piper's alternate-history SF novel *Gunpowder God* isn't so successful when you substitute sodium-nitrate fertilizer for saltpetre. The result is too damp (can you say hygroscopic?). Nice fireworks, no bang.

• In those days it was still possible to buy tall yellow tins of calcium carbide at the Newport branch of the motorists' shop Halford's. This was meant for old-fashioned acetylene bicycle lamps. Drop a lump into water and acetylene gas comes bubbling out, along with smelly impurities. A carefully planned experiment determined beyond reasonable doubt that if a scientific investigator drops carbide into all the inkwells and fills his classroom with a terrible stench, he gets caned.

• John Dickson Carr's locked-room mystery *The Hollow Man* mentions the ingredients of the 'Krupp preparation' – that is, thermite – but experimental science was unable to buy them in Newport, not even at the largest Boots the Chemist. (That Carr novel was pressed on me by my favourite aunt, Louise, who also introduced me to *The Day of the Triffids*, *Catch-22* and mulligatawny soup. Alas, she died far too young.)

• The recipe for nitrogen tri-iodide or NI_3 in *Farnham's Freehold* by Robert A. Heinlein (another SF novel) can be improved upon by using solid iodine crystals from the Newport High School labs. This was a traditional discovery made by most chemistry classes even without Heinlein's help. The resulting contact explosive is liable to detonate without any assistance whatever, but if you keep it wet enough it can first be smeared on floors, blackboards, desks and anywhere else you fancy. When victims touch or step on it, there are exciting mini-explosions and puffs of purple smoke. Roars of laughter! Breaks the ice at parties! A definite triumph for Science.

• It was not possible to confirm the spectacular pyrotechnics produced by dropping large lumps of sodium into water (as described many years later in Gene Wolfe's *The Book of the New Sun*) because the authorities kept the school supply too well locked up. And the even more excitingly reactive potassium as well. We all agreed this was shockingly distrustful.

SENTIMENTAL MARCHING SONG

In the barber shop
In the game
In the lair of the wrinkled old worm
All men the same
Born to brutalize on every scale
Passing down the iron line
Cocooned in a fist
Running through the tension rods
    never kissed
So stop all that moaning and sing
Along with the sirens outside
I'll be over at ten
We can take a ride
The beast lurches into the road
Breathing deep
Buckets of brains
Rooms full of sleep
He needs a little love at closing time

aside by the general reader, as so much trash belonging to the
worst school of Bedlam literature – since he seems not so much
unable to learn as disdainful of learning the craft of an artist.
   —Henry F. Chorley, in the *Athenaeum* (London), Oct. 25, 1851

Flipper agrees with the man from the *Athenaeum*. She liked
the movie better. She's been reading the book to me (from
memory of course) for years, bit by bit, and she's pretty sick of
it. She only perseveres because I'm in it. One day, she hopes,
it will all come back to me. I find it totally impenetrable. We
wonder if anybody in the world has ever sat down and read
the whole thing straight through. I can't really tell if the mad
(rather than bad) English belongs to the book or if it's just
Flipper's translation. Dolphins do have an accent and her
constant re-telling of the story may have added some weird
Chinese whisper filter that has distorted its whole factual
basis beyond all recognition. Maybe it wasn't really me?
Maybe it wasn't a whale at all?

     Sometimes we stop reading the book and make up our
own versions. They are usually shorter and funnier:

One cold Christmas night the grumpy, obsessive manager
of the Peapod vegetarian restaurant is sitting all alone. He's
watching re-runs of Matlock *on his tiny black-and-white TV*
and eating a stale alfalfa-sprout sandwich when he hears
someone knocking very lightly on his front door. There's a
blizzard raging outside and as he opens the door thick flakes
of snow come blowing into the restaurant and stick to his

THE LAST COUNT

If I was looking for trouble
I know a place or two
And a hundred was to even up
    the score
A dozen ways to beat the devil
No matter how the dice might fall
But at the last count there's
    nothing I want at all

How many times did you sit alone
    staring at the door
I can't count those days on one
    hand
I'd need three or four
And how many nights did I sit
    and drink

'til the big one slipped away
Half past drinks at half price eight

It's 1 2 3 falling
5 6 7 hate myself

So play another number, it's only
    half past one
And I'm a fraction of the person
    that you once counted on
At the last count my days are
    numbered
Chalked up on the wall
At the last count there's nothing I
    want at all

eyebrows and beard. He looks back and forth but can't see anyone and he's about to shut the door when a tiny voice says, 'I'm down here!' He looks down and sees a white snail on his doorstep. 'Hello and Merry Christmas,' says the white snail, 'Can I come in and share some of your Christmas cheer? It's very cold out here and I have nowhere to go.' The manager of the Peapod picks up the white snail and throws him as far as he can out into the freezing snowstorm. One year later, on Christmas night, he's still alone, watching the same TV show and eating what's left of another stale old sandwich. Suddenly he hears someone knocking and, once again, when he opens the door there's nobody there. He peers out into the blizzard and is just about to shut the door when a tiny voice from down below says, 'What did you do that for?' – THE END.

Flipper also used to tell a story about Ray Bradbury going into Starbuck's, but I don't get it.

MIGRATION FATIGUE

'You got to keep moving, Blondie,' screeches Flipper, just as I'm nodding off. She swims round and round my hump in neat concentric spirals, leaving a trail of perfect little bubbles in her wake. 'There, I confess, a nice halo for Virgin Whitey! Ha ha! Wakey, wakey! Can't stop now.' I know, I've trudged round this planet's oceans for nearly two hundred years and I'm ready to retire. Where the hell are we, anyway? Flipper thinks you should never travel by the same route twice. 'Think up new ways always, new directions, fire up the dry bone

F.... All too much of my maths homework at Newport High School consisted of playing drinking games in a smoky pub. The beer was some foul carbonated slop of the late sixties (Courage Worst? Double Diamond?), costing one shilling and fourpence a pint, and the game of **FIZZ-BUZZ** was a reliable way to choke it down.

If you are very lucky, you won't have met it. We mathematical scholars would sit round a table in the Amputee's Arms, counting in turn, clockwise round the ring. *One. Two. Three.* At five, and every multiple of five, you don't say the number but shout *Fizz!* At seven and its multiples the word is *Buzz!* – and the order of play reverses direction. Anyone making a mistake must take a huge swig from his beer (amateur rules), drain the glass and buy another (tournament rules), or knock back any drinks in front of him and buy a round (insane idiot rules).

Unfortunately we got too good at it. Even the double thrill of *Fizz Buzz!* at multiples of 35 began to lose its edge. So I and my mate Dai Price started attaching electrodes to the traditional rules. One early experiment, which even the slow-witted could handle, was to add *Oink!* as the (ahem) buzzword for multiples of three. Daio developed a particularly obscene *Oink!* whose mere sound came under the heading of gamesmanship. The corpse of the rotten game began to twitch slightly.

Burp! for multiples of 11 was the next logical addition. By now we were sweating, concentrating intently, and falling over much sooner than usual (see above, Tournament Rules). Next: *Clang!* whenever the count reached a prime number. It was around this stage that I stopped remembering trivia like closing times or how I'd got home afterwards. The final blows to sanity were *Pow!* for perfect squares and *Zap!* for powers of two.

By now, the intelligent reader will see, there were no bloody landmarks. Pale, strained faces ringed the table, soddenly trying to follow a count which instead of *One Two Three Four* began *Clang Pow! Clang Zap! Oink Clang! Pow Zap!* The supreme moment of triumph came when, or if, we galloped into the straight with *Oink Buzz! Burp! Clang! Oink! Fizz Pow!* . . . and then at last the first number that came through in clear: *Twenty-six!*

I'm not sure what the other pub regulars thought of us, but they used to look worried.

synapses,' she says, 'Drive that car home from work the same way every night and you'll be getting brain rot, then crash, wallop, dead!' She looks down her beak at all the millions who journey as slaves to instinct, hunger and yearnings.

THE FILMING OF MOBY DICK IN YOUGHAL

Death to Moby Dick, signed Gregory Peck
In and out of his make-up
With a whale-bone for a leg
And the little bar down by the quayside
Was a gold mine every day
Just like sitting on an oil well
When the motion-picture people came to stay
White whaler, black heart
Out there hunting with the hounds
Caught much more with a camera
Panned across the faces of the people hanging round
So all the local were extras and all the locals got paid
There's no acting in the flat black eyes
Of old women as the Pequod sailed away
40 summers dived out of reach
And on a TV round the back
We've got a picture on a videotape
Of the big fish that never came back
So far from the heart of Europe
The young left long ago
To look for work in London
Boston and Chicago

PILL SAILOR

A pit bull tattoo
One good eye of blue
That's wandering still
But what can you do
These ropes are all knotted and
　　tangled round me
I'm a sailor who wandered a little
　　too far from the sea

Did they raise up this child just to
　　die
To stare for too long into one sky
Shirley Bassey's from Tiger Bay
But I spend my nights down in Pill
They shut down the docks
Thrown our lives on the rocks
But my good eye's wandering still
Past the pubs where I festered all
　　day
Transporter bridge, transport me
　　away
'Cos these ropes are all knotted and
　　tangled round me
I'm a sailor who wandered a little
　　too far from the sea

They passed in the channel great ships
　　by the score
To carry out coal and to carry in ore
And at night these old sea legs were
　　anxious to stray
They'd come from all over but never
　　intended to stay
So tell me something I don't know
And find me a skipper with somewhere
　　to go

'I've got a bone to pick with you,' David Williams, Burlington choirboy and merchant seaman, tells me. 'That song 'Pill Sailor' – I've done every word of that, taking the ore into Newport and all that . . . but Shirley Bassey's not from Tiger Bay. *I'm* from there, but she's from Splott!"

G...

The **GAER**, also known to locals as the Gollars, was the perfect place for kids to muck around, stalk each other through ancient, bracken-infested earthworks, and – if you tried really hard – get lost. It's actually an Iron Age hill fort on the west side of Newport, overlooking Tredegar Park and the Ebbw River. In our day it also overlooked a golf course, now vanished under horrid new housing developments. A 2006 BBC report insisted on calling it the Tredegar Hillfort, but Newportonians will have no truck with this blatant revisionism. It's the Gaer.

We grew up on the edge of the then-quite-new Gaer Estate, a sprawl of modern houses, flats and prefabs next to the Gaer itself. The Gaer School loomed large in our lives, and Jon's was the first christening held at the new church St Martin in the Gaer. Afterwards, it had to be consecrated again.

The Gaer Estate was a kind of literary time capsule, with all its roads named for writers. Street names were handed out in strict order of the planners' idea of their importance, working down from the very long Shakespeare Crescent through Dickens Drive, Ben Jonson Way, Masefield Vale (John Masefield was Poet Laureate at the time), Ruskin Rise and Kipling Hill. I always hoped that Morton Way was a nod to the humorist J.B. 'Beachcomber' Morton, but probably they meant H.V. the travel writer. Hacks with lower ratings got Groves – Brontë, Pepys, Shaw – or Gardens, like Barrie, Macaulay and Marlowe. Right at the bottom of the pecking order were the small fry who were fobbed off with mere Closes, from Jane Austen to H.G. Wells. Rather daringly for that era, one Close was named for the notoriously filthy James Joyce.

Drinkwater Close always seemed to be an odd one out, but at secondary school one of the English teachers explained all by making us read a particularly gloomy poem by the now-forgotten John Drinkwater. 'Long time in some forgotten churchyard earth of Warwickshire / My fathers in their generations . . .' had, to cut a long story short, snuffed it. What mysterious pull did *he* have with the Gaer planners?

Naturally the tiniest and most insignificant of all the Closes – as far as I can make out on the

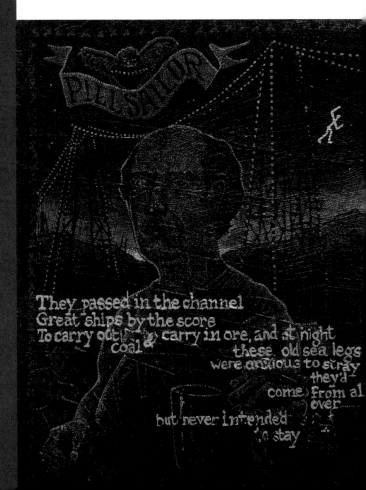

They passed in the channel
Great ships by the score
To carry out coal & carry in ore, and at night
these old sea legs
were anxious to stray
they'd
come from all
over
but never intended
to stay

In 1954 we went on a trip to the Irish Sea, just Flipper and me. There's a little port town just east of Cork called Youghal, where John Huston, the famous Hollywood movie director, was making a film of the book. He wanted to film it there so he could go fox-hunting on his days off. It was a long way for us to go for a movie but Flipper was still a pretty good navigator back then. An actor called Gregory Peck played the old Captain, tottering around on a fake-whalebone leg looking more like Abe Lincoln than anyone else. Flipper says Peck is the perfect name for an actor who plays a man who is in fact an egg with a baby chick inside.

We swam fairly aimlessly just outside the harbor walls and nobody ever spotted us. Not even when I was lying there, logging in the warm Gulf Stream waters, during those long boring gaps between takes. That was the first time I noticed the shiny thing stuck through Flipper's fin. She caught me staring at it through the snot-green seawater. 'Don't worry, Snow-cone, it's germ-free.'

I never found out who they got to play me. That was all filmed somewhere else. The crew and cast all stayed at Paddy's Hotel and signed publicity photos for Paddy the owner, who had them mounted and framed and hung on the wall of the bar to remind everyone who came in for a drink that this was the last thing that was ever going to happen in that town. Flipper says Paddy got it all wrong, and things in Youghal are definitely on the up and up. Paddy's Hotel (which was called Moby Dick's for most of the '80s and '90s) has been converted into an Eastern European electro-fun pub called Albino's.

WHITER SHADE OF WHALE

There's a nasty-tasting lake in the country of Mexico where the fish walk around on little legs. They are called axolotl and are prone to albinism. Their bodies are long and ghostly white, while their lungs stick out of their heads like bloody red feathers. Due to something chemical that's lacking in the lake, they never turn into what they're meant to turn into and have learned to fuck and make babies without ever reaching puberty. They can be horny irresponsible tweenagers forever. Flipper finds this all quite admirable, but the fact they eat their babies and have managed to hang onto their legs creeps us out.

  I'm an albino whale and I'm not unique in this. My eyes aren't pink like a ferret's or a lab rat's; they're more of a violet color. I just lack pigment. Flipper taught me a great comeback (dolphin wit and repartee!) if anyone bugs me about this: 'You may have the deeper ink hole but I have the biggest pen.' I haven't had a chance to use it on anyone yet. Like any other whale I'm a just a giant floating warehouse packed to the lungs with blubber and oil and waxy aromatic ambergris but no jolly whalin' lad's ever going to hunt me down for my melanin.

  Apparently my albinism

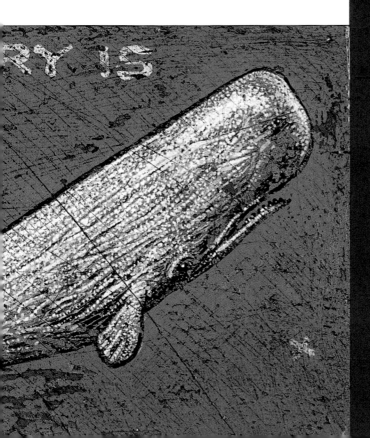

map – was allotted to a literary critic: Hazlitt. This was inspirational. I went on to become an insignificant book reviewer, though of science fiction rather than drama.

Shakespeare? Oh yes, he wrote some plays, but if you grew up in the Gaer he was mainly celebrated as a Crescent.

H.... Mrs Saunders was the first of my **HEAD TEACHERS** she ran a tiny dame-school in the back sitting room of her house in Melfort Road, where I first grappled with key sentences like 'Dan is a man' and 'The fat nag ran to the gap.' Lessons were punctuated by disaster clean-up operations when this narrative excitement became too much for infant bladders. Mrs Saunders regularly threatened chair-wetters with a dose from her feared red bottle of 'Wakey-Uppy Medicine", understood to be an experience too awful to contemplate. It was in her classes that I first met my buddy Martin Hoare, who went on to be a year ahead of me at the Gaer School, at Newport High, and at Brasenose in Oxford – and for blackmail purposes remembers all about the Saunders Academy, curse him. When in 1998 I travelled to Minneapolis to be a guest of honour at the local science fiction convention, my hostess Geri Sullivan had been briefed by Martin to place a terrifying bottle labelled 'Wakey-Uppy Medicine' at my bedside. It turned out to be sherry.

Our own Aunt Ol (technically Great-Aunt Olive) was the reigning headmistress of Gaer Junior School in those days, but retired before I got there, and spent the following decades ruling the family rather than the school with her famous rod of iron. Almost all I remember about her Gaer replacement Mr Griffiths was that he kept a special library of treasured books for advanced readers, including most of Hugh Lofting's *Doctor Dolittle* saga. I caught the fantasy habit young.

The other thing about Mr Griffiths that sticks in my mind was our father's explanation of the important difference between him and D. Parry Michael of Newport High School, where I was about to start. 'For four years you've had a headmaster whose head looks as though it's been squashed *this* way.' Dad's hands moved together, miming side-to-side pressure. 'Your new one's head looks as though it's been squashed *that* way.' Same business, but top to bottom. In this way I was prepared for various canings by D. Parry Michael, though not for the fan letter he sent about one of my books in the mid-1980s.

DPM had brought a touch of public-school tradition to Newport High by dividing us up into houses named for the rivers of Monmouthshire: Monnow, Severn, Usk and Wye. No one was allowed to be in Gryffindor. There wasn't much deadly rivalry, although in addition to sports (rugby, rugby, rugby, swimming and rugby) the houses were pitted against each other in an annual Eisteddfod where earnest girls with tragic voices invariably recited Dylan Thomas's 'And Death Shall Have No Dominion". Attendance was compulsory, and would-be poets gave up their ambitions on the spot.

School classes had arbitrary letters to avoid any trace of elitism – N, H, S and M for Newport High School, Mon. – but secretly N and H were the fast stream with the other two reserved for clods. In my fourth year (4N, he mentioned smugly), an English teacher blew the gaff. Some duplicated sets of test papers were so badly fixed together, with a stapler on the 'pin' setting, that they disintegrated while being handed out. 'Well,' said our mentor in tones of utmost contempt, 'these seem to have been stapled by 4S . . .'

Incidentally, most of the Newport High masters and mistresses still wore black academic gowns, just as in *Stalky & Co.* or Billy Bunter. Tell that to today's youngsters and they won't believe you.

I . . . For several years, among the Croesyceiliog family and friends especially, there was a fashion for surreal ornamental globs that stood in empty fireplaces or were proudly displayed on window-sills. They came in various shapes and sizes but all had a runny, molten-plastic look, as though Salvador Dali had been preparing a huge soft watch but forgot to turn off the oven until far too late. In fact these artforms were solidified lumps of nylon slag left over from the arcane **INDUSTRIAL PROCESSES** at British Nylon Spinners, where our Uncle Bryn worked. Great-Uncle Bryn really: his wife Aunty Rosie was one of the three weird sisters Hilda, Lenta and Rosie, of whom Lenta was our mother's mother and also our Grandmother Len. Bryn was also a useful source of raw material for family knitters: all the children were parcelled

BUTTER SONG

Very very
Butter better very well
Butcher, whether it will sel[l]
Well is well and silver sells
Sell a salted almond to Nel[l]
That she will accept, and
    then
What does a fatty do?
She does not pay for it
No she does not
She does not pay for it
By this time they've learne[d]
    how to spell
Very very likely the whole
    thing
Is extraordinary
Which is a great relief
All the time her name is
    Marguerite Ida

J . . . is also for **JOHN CALE**, I should add. (Or should it be C?) I first heard 'Half Past France' down at the Folk Club in Pill but never noticed the Velvet Underground 'til my first day in Leeds in 1976, when founding Mekon Andy Corrigan told me his mates in the Fine Art Department had formed a band (look at us!) that was a cross between Doctor Feelgood and the Velvets. Feelgood I was well familiar with – short songs, short hair, they sorta stood out in the mid '70s. Imagine my surprise years later when my parents' neighbor Mrs King asks me if I was still playing music in America and if perhaps I know her cousin in New York. I'd known her since I was ten but it took her 25 years to tell me her cousin was John Cale. Turns out Joan and Edgar King had been backstage at the Reading Festival for the VU reunion. 'Llew was very friendly really,' says Edgar. 'John said he might not be, but he was very nice.'—JL

up in scratchy but indestructible nylon sweaters. Indestructible, that is, until they met their first burning cigarette-end.

Len's husband Arthur worked at the Avondale Tinplate Works (so indeed did Len herself) and brought home odd little machined bearings and cams, not big enough to stand impressively on the mantelpiece. When I took a vacation job at the Gwent Alcan works in 1974, I wondered whether I'd be continuing the family tradition by coming home with pockets full of small aluminium trinkets. In the event my services were in demand because the factory shop gave workers huge discounts on cooking foil.

I was stacking aluminium sheets at Alcan when the Thames Valley Police tracked me down and appeared on the shop floor to nick me for setting off loud bangs in Oxford that summer. The foreman was disgusted that one of his least promising young workers had found this paltry excuse to down tools early. 'You skiving sod,' he said as the constabulary led me away.

J . . . A brother of mine, almost exactly four and a half years younger. See practically any page of this book. The age gap between me and my 'tiny little deformed brother' (a phrase whose origin is lost in the mists of alcohol) kept us well apart at school. One later anecdote, just one: during my final year at Oxford, **JON** came to a party at the sordid college lodgings in New Inn Hall Street. There was much home-made beer, I remember, from extensive brewing operations in a disused cellar kept nicely warm by the central-heating boiler. There were rust-spotted Watneys Party Seven tins that never got opened but went the rounds of student parties as revered cargo-cult goods. There was a sinister punch concocted from fortified fruit wines and other sticky ingredients, in a plastic dustbin from the home-brew operation . . .

The last of these was Jon's downfall. As the party wound down and the punch sank to low tide, he hefted the bin with both hands to take a mighty swig. Some passing physicist – not me, I promise – helpfully raised the far end a few inches. Jon vanished in a wave of murky fluid and fruit bits. The grisly aftermath came in the small hours, as a limbless monstrosity inched and humped its way about the building like some protoplasmic horror from the works of Arthur Machen. When eventually I mustered the courage to turn on a light, the crawling abomination proved to be Jon – still sticky all over and unable to get loose from the sleeping bag. Perhaps, if we hadn't ripped him free of his cocoon, he would have metamorphosed into a lovely butterfly.

The moral, probably, is 'don't drink from dustbins.'

K... ■ KINGSWAY CENTRE

They weren't called shopping malls back then, but the KINGSWAY CENTRE was Newport's first manifestation of the wave of extraordinarily bad town planning that swept over South Wales in the 1960s. The chief architectural merit of the Centre is that it gives me something to put against K in this alphabet. The Kingsway Centre has no other architectural merits.

Newport's main consolation was that the Centre wasn't quite as dire as the pedestrian shopping complex in Cwmbran New Town, whose designers had got the plans mixed up with blueprints for a wind tunnel. Hellish gales blew down the long bare arcades, spawning whirlwinds and dust devils. Until the council added a complex system of baffles and spoilers, little old ladies who dared to put up an umbrella in Cwmbran were regularly recovered by mountain rescue teams from the higher slopes of Twmbarlwm.

L... ■ LANGFORD

There's nothing very exciting about the family name. It's irremediably English, a 'locational surname' for people who happened to live in one of the places called LANGFORD or Longford in Bedfordshire, Devonshire, Essex, Norfolk, Nottinghamshire, Oxfordshire, Somerset and Wiltshire (most of them recorded in Domesday Book). Not many Welsh counties in that lot. And it doesn't mean anything more thrilling than 'the long shallow river crossing", the long or lang (Old English *langa*) ford.

We are probably not connected to the first recorded specimen, Osm' de Langeford, who was listed in the Pipe Rolls for Wiltshire in 1130. By an uncanny coincidence, though, the first computer on which I did serious programming was an IBM 1130!

At school, until a teacher's curse fell on me

symbolizes different things to different people, who in turn project their lurid obsessions on the blank white screen of my hide. My parents' hides were a sort of blue-grey color, but there was never any question as to my paternity. Aside from the Captain, the paleness just hasn't been a problem, although I understand how it might be tougher in less tolerant social situations. Down in the deep, where the sunlight dims, we don't see color anyway. In the Gulf, by Galveston, you can't see a bloody thing – it's like swimming in a bouillabaisse. Things just bump into you and slide over your tail and fins anonymously. In the clear crystal shallows by the reef everybody's dazzling and gorgeous, and while we're happy to eat each other without compunction, nobody thinks they're better than anyone else because of their skin color. That would be stupid.

Flipper says casting an albino as the villain in a book or a movie has become a total cliché. She gives various examples that mean nothing to me, adding enigmatically, 'That *Da Vinci Cod* was a stinking load of wallop.' She's my little mine of information.

NO RETURN TO THE DEEP

Here, as I lie on the muddy tidal banks of the Severn estuary, I can see two great bridges spanning the divide just up the river. The hippies keep trying to push me into deeper water, back into the safety of myth and mystery, but I'm not co-operating. They have ropes and long, pointy prodding tools and pathetic little rubber boats that I could pop like puffer fish if I had half a mind to. But I don't need to do anything to resist their efforts; I'm well and truly stuck.

So near but yet so far. I am half in this world, half in that, and I'm completely washed up. Curiosity got the better of me, too, but after all the good and the bad, the fast and the loose, the damp and the dry (not to mention several hundred pages of dense black & white), who could really blame me? Well, that's obvious, isn't it? It seems like he always had it in for me.

I PREFER CAPTAIN MORGAN

He was never my favorite sea captain anyway. I prefer Captain Morgan. We used to come across these fantastic little pictures of him, stuck to bottles. He stands there, smirking evilly with his barrel and his sword, all dressed up in red and gold. I love his lacy white cuffs and frilly neck scarf. That's a *real* sea captain. The bottles we found were down at the bottom of this lovely warm lagoon over by the reef. It was quite a squeeze for us to get in there. They nestled in the soft white sand, gleaming and glinting like treasure. They'd probably fallen from some roaring pleasure craft (the ones that nick my fins and hide with their puny propellers) or been thrown from this place Flipper knew, called the sundeck of Cap'n A's Crab Shack.

One day, far out in open water, I saw a bottle of Captain Morgan Spiced Rum floating on the surface. It had a piece of paper inside. Flipper said it must have been a message, a message in a bottle. I wondered what it said, but I had no hands to get the top off with – and no way to read it even if I'd grasped the whole concept. I still wonder who it was from and imagine

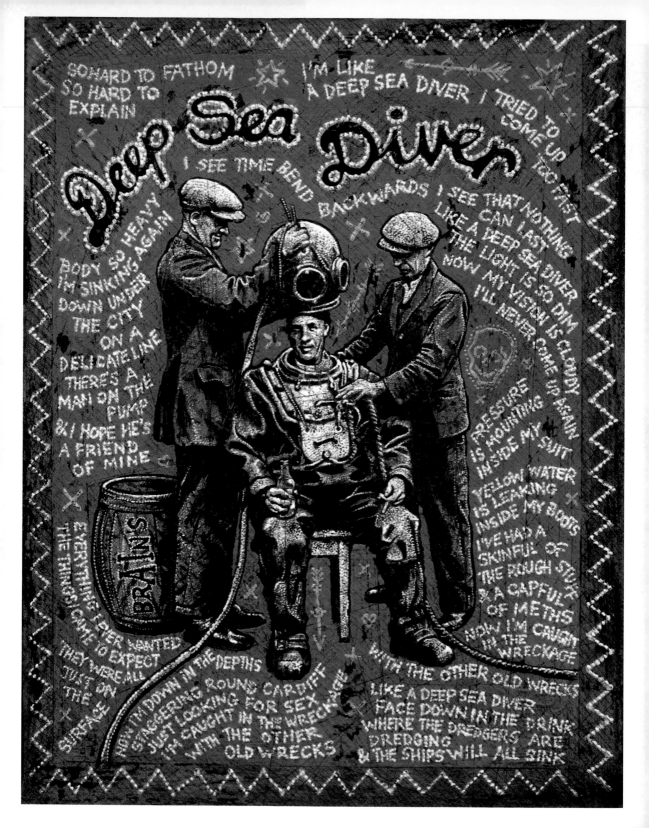

44

DEEP SEA DIVER

So hard to fathom
So hard to explain
Body so heavy I'm sinking again.
Down under the city
On a delicate line, there's a man on the pump
And I hope he's a friend of mine

Everything I ever wanted
The things I came to expect
they were all just on the surface
And now I'm down in the depths
Staggering round Cardiff
Just looking for sex
I'm caught in the wreckage
With the other old wrecks

Like a deep sea diver
I tried to come up too fast
I see time bend backwards
I see that nothing can last
Like a deep sea diver
The light is so dim
Now my vision is cloudy
I'll never come up again

Pressure is mounting inside my suit
Yellow water is oozing inside my boots
I've had a skinful of the rough stuff
And a capful of meths
Now I'm caught in the wreckage
With the other old wrecks

Like a deep sea diver
I tried to come up too fast
I see time bend backwards
I see that nothing can last
Like a deep sea diver
Face down in the drink
Where the dredgers are dredging
And the ships will all sink

(see Woodwork), they tended to say Lanky Langford because I was tall and thin. I'm still reasonably tall despite natural shrinkage, but for some reason that nickname never occurs to anybody nowadays. Happily, the universal tendency to misspell Langford as Longford has faded since the once notorious Lord Longford took himself away to investigate that great porn-shop in the sky. But people still try to cheer us up by sending photos of the village sign at Hanging Langford (Salisbury, Wilts). Wishful thinking, no doubt.

Notable anagrams include Alfgrond the Viking berserker, a greasy-spoon Chinese restaurant called Fong Lard, and that dread villain of many a fantasy trilogy, the Fanglord. My publications list includes a booklet titled *Wrath of the Fanglord*, which may have been a bad idea.

Mum's side of the family provides all the Welshness, including a seething mass of Evanses who tended to marry other Evanses in hope of making life as difficult as possible for amateur genealogists. You should hear the grumbles from my wife Hazel, who is an amateur genealogist.

M. . . Supernatural-fiction author **ARTHUR MACHEN** was born and raised in Caerleon, just up the road from Newport, and in 2007 they unveiled a sculpture there to mark the sixtieth anniversary of his death. It was also the eightieth anniversary of H.P. Lovecraft's essay 'Supernatural Horror in Literature' (1927), which gave our local boy an enthusiastic plug: 'Of living creators of cosmic fear raised to its most artistic pitch, few if any can hope to equal the versatile Arthur Machen, author of some dozen tales long and short, in which the elements of hidden horror and brooding fright attain an almost incomparable substance and realistic acuteness.' This was Lovecraft's generous way of saying, 'I'm planning to pinch Machen's best effects.'

What we need now is the Arthur Machen Experience as a Caerleon tourist magnet. Careful research should reveal the exact chair in the King's Arms or Ship Inn where, after a few too many beers, the author dissolved into 'a dark and putrid mass, seething with corruption and hideous rottenness, neither liquid nor solid' – and thus got the inspiration for his gruesome tale 'The Novel of the White Powder". (Please note that the ominous White Powder is taken dissolved in water, and not snorted.) Perhaps one of the Roman antiquities in Caerleon museum inspired the golden treasure brought from under the mountain in Machen's story 'The Red Hand' – an ornament so revoltingly obscene that people cry out, 'Put it away, man; hide it, for Heaven's sake, hide it!' (It is known as the Pain of the Goat. Suitable reconstructions should sell like hot cakes in the souvenir shop.) There would be excursions to Wentwood to view ill-omened glades exactly like the one where the hellspawned little girl of *The Great God Pan* was seen playing on the grass with a 'strange naked man' whom the observer was 'unable to describe more fully.' See also the entries for Cardiff and Sheep.

Langford links: Our Newport High School headmaster D. Parry Michael wrote a learned monograph about Arthur Machen that was published by the University of Wales Press. Croesy-ceilog, where Grandmother Len and her close family lived, features in AM's nasty story of abduction and sacrifice by the Little People, 'The Shining Pyramid". One of the family treasures is a letter handwritten by Machen to a Mr Snelling – apparently a pal of Grandfather 'Pop' Langford's – in 1937.

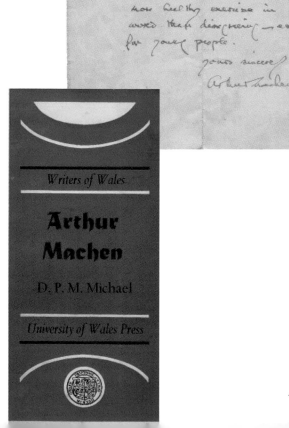

Writers of Wales

Arthur Machen

D. P. M. Michael

University of Wales Press

N... is for **NOXIOUS**.

is for **NOXIOUS**. Well, Newport would have been a bit too obvious, wouldn't it?

For this episode, I think *The Observer's Book of Common Fungi* must bear full responsibility. There never seemed to be any common fungi in our garden, but once upon a time on a visit to what I believe was the Forest of Dean, I was fascinated to find some slightly uncommon ones. They had such an unusual shape that I could actually recognize them from the picture in the book. As a rule identification was far from easy, with instructions like: 'Apply a dilute solution of Culpepper's what it said.

Flipper says Captain Morgan was a very bad man – a monster, perhaps. Not just a guy on a billboard designed to sell you some spiced-up fantasy lifestyle, but a real pirate who did terrible, bloodthirsty things and totally got away with it. 'All the other pirate people got hung up,' Flipper confided, 'but Morgan went straight legit, built a state-of-the-home in a new port and spawned a dynasty. A long tall home for his monster family.'

'And where might that be?'

'Far over the second big ocean, in the land of the Whales,' she replied.

'We have our own country? Why didn't you tell me before?"

'Sorry Ski-slope, I diddle know you were from anywhere at all.'

'Tell me, Dolphin – is it only monsters that live there?'

HERE BE MONSTERS

It's cool to be cast as the anti-hero, but I'm not really a vengeful monster. I can't see anything of myself in that depiction at all. All the weird, biblical, supernatural crap was just the Captain, right? I told Flipper about my doubts. 'Look, if that all had really happened, you'd think some of it would have stuck in my mind?"

'Ahem, it may not be your mind it got stuck in,' clicked Flipper with some amusement. She'd been reading the book to me for over a month and we'd barely got to New Bedford. 'Oh ye of lethal faith! You need some evidence, is it? I'll get you solid

GREEN VALLEYS

We laugh through trouble
You've got to be a joker
Couldn't be more honest
Couldn't get much broker

It's better, or so we've been told
To do nothing than haul another load of coal
Green valleys and life on the dole
Make nothing and pour it down an empty hole

The force of nature
Obeys the master
Gets crazier and crazier
I was born and raised here

Old machinery, haul it away
Shopping centers, rolls of astro-
    turf to lay
Incentives, bribes to be paid
Juggle figures in the capital so far
    away

Here comes the saviour
He's a man in a blazer
Investment failure
I was born and raised here

It's better, or so we've been told
To do nothing than haul another
    load of coal
Green valleys and life on the dole
Make nothing and pour it down
    an empty hole

The flickering twilight
Holds a strange fascination
We'll be rubber-necking
At the death of a nation

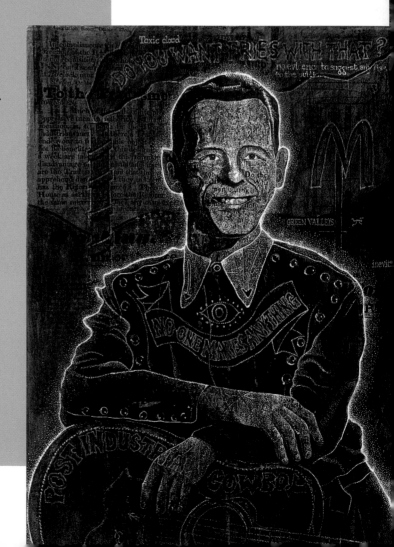

49

I'm lazy but what can I do
Oooh nothing, I only want to be with you
Time lately is going askew
Green valleys, I only want to be with you

It's better, or so we've been told
To do nothing than haul another load of coal
Green valleys and life on the dole
Make nothing and pour it down an empty hole
Do nothing and pour it down an empty hole
Have nothing and pour it down an empty hole

proof and about time, too,' she whelped, swimming off down the length of my gnarly white haunches. I cranked my deep set eye-ball round to see where she was going but she soon disappeared under my tail.

After about five minutes I felt a strange tickling sensation very far away that made me want to breach, but within a few seconds it was gone, and when Flipper appeared again she was gripping a rusty harpoon between her multitude of tiny sharp teeth. It was attached to six or seven feet of rotten, tangled rope that had clearly been severed with violent force. 'This sharpie old thing must have been stuck in your butt ending for somewhat over 160 years,' she smirked, slapping her fins together soundlessly. 'Are we having a lion's Dan moment yet?' I told her I couldn't handle any more biblical references right now.

All along, Flipper had been completely convinced of my true identity and had explored the cracks and furrows of my chalky vastness with diligence and admirable sensitivity, until she found the object of her search protruding from my aft regions. 'Looky here, Snowball,' she said, gesticulating with her snout, 'It says in little brass letters: Property of the Pequod. That's the right one then, isn't it?' Proof enough, I suppose, except I can't read. I mean, it could have said *Welcome to Jamaica. Please Drive Carefully,* for all I know.

There are plenty of real monsters out there in the heaving dark oceans of this world. You don't circumnavigate the globe at enormous depths for hundreds of years without running into a whole gallery of complete bastards.

Take the hagfish, for starters. It likes to bore its way up your back passage and eat you from the inside out, choicest organs first. The only beast ever with a skull but no spine, it swarms in frenzied packs and squirts out a viscous silicate paste from glandular nodules all up and down its ugly phallic shaft that thickens alarmingly on contact with water and chokes anything that attempts to prey on it. Then it ties itself in a disgusting knot, which it proceeds to run lasciviously down its entire length to clean off. It has teeth on its tongue and palate and no sense of humor or poetry. It hasn't evolved for hundreds of millions of years. It hasn't needed to; it's a perfect monster.

I bet you've never even seen a colossal squid, either, let alone wrestled one for three days in fifteen fathoms of freezing salt water. Try to imagine thirty-foot-long writhing tentacles that don't just throttle you with sucker cups the size of toilet plungers, but hack into your flesh with vicious swiveling hooks that can pivot 360 degrees for maximum ripping and gripping. Then there's the flat, dead eyes (as big as basketballs) that stare you down all blank and cold, while the monster tries to squeeze your guts right out of your blow holes. They're tough, but if you weren't meant to eat them, why do they taste so good!

I'm big and old and white and ugly, but I'm not a monster. And I won't be your scapegoat or your bogeyman anymore, either. I know how much you need monsters to sustain all your bullshit dry earth schemes, but I wish you'd just leave me out of it, OK? Watch out, I'm going to blow!

Alkali to the gills. If the resulting coloration is lemon-yellow, the fungus is Common Blewit, delicious when fried in lard. If canary-yellow, it is the lethally poisonous False Newtbane . . .'

The unusual shape of my specimen fungi was very rude indeed. They were exceedingly male. They were in fact the Dog Stinkhorn, and I gathered some to take home and gloat over. Perhaps I could persuade the spores to grow in our garden! With a slight sigh of resignation, Dad stowed them in the boot of the car and off we drove. But not very far.

You would not believe what an astonishing stench a few Dog Stinkhorns can generate inside a closed car in just a few minutes. We pulled up hastily. The priceless botanical specimens were chucked into a ditch. Mum waved her perfume bottle around with wild abandon. It helped, but she insists she's been unable to wear Chanel No 5 ever since, because of the terrible memory. Even a tiny whiff still conjures up that very rude smell. I blame *The Observer's Book of Common Fungi.*

O . . . Poets have struggled for centuries to find a rhyme for **ORANGE**, and according to popular wisdom there just isn't one. One of my favourite dead American authors, James Branch Cabell, wrote a story called 'The Rhyme for Porringer"; much later, the living SF author Michael Swanwick took his cue from Cabell and came up with the back-formation 'porringe".

As any South Walian knows, the true rhyme is The Blorenge – a hill just south of Abergavenny.

P . . . Our first dog, **PUNCH**, was always tactfully referred to as a black Labrador. Other breeds had gone into the mix, though: he wasn't broad or tall enough to manage a truly convincing Labrador impersonation. Punch furiously defended the garden of our Burnfort Road house against the forces of evil, which for some reason took the form of little old ladies. Men with black masks, striped vests and large bags labelled SWAG could come and go as they liked, in danger only of being joyfully licked to death, but the little old ladies who menaced the Langford household tended to get bitten. Mum had a special Christmas list of victims who needed to be sent apologetic cards and choccies each year.

This was all uncannily similar to the situation in James Thurber's 'The Dog That Bit People' (in *A Second Century of Humour*, illustrated by Fougasse, one of the books I remember being on the Langford shelves when I first learned to read). Unlike Thurber's fearsome hound, Punch never bit the family . . . well, except just once. He followed me to the Gaer Junior School one day and got into a fight with another dog in the playground. Showing my immense native power of stupidity, I tried to separate them. Shortly afterwards came the exciting new experience of getting my hand stitched up in the Royal Gwent, followed by my first tetanus injection. Another rite of passage for the Hero with a Thousand Embarrassments.

Jon adds an episode which has utterly vanished from my own memory: 'the time we took Punch down to the post office on Bassaleg Road and he bit some grumpy old vicar and you (with great presence of mind) did not hesitate to lie to him (A VICAR!) about both our identities and address . . . I have always admired you for that one act sir – though the horror of the vicar rolling up his trouser leg to show the grizzly blue black bloody bruise on his translucent white shin flesh still haunts my midnite slumbers!"

When Punch and Burnfort Road were long gone, we had Bella the pedigree basset hound – Jon's dog really – and sort of accidentally acquired Heidi the mostly-Jack-Russell. Bella was the brains of this outfit, a Napoleon of foodcrime. Kitchen surfaces that neither of them could reach alone were conquered by, according to the best guesses of forensic science, Heidi standing on Bella's back for a desperate leap. Either that or Mum's special party dish of sausage meat in pastry, something like a gigantic sausage roll infused with onions, was abducted by Alien Grays.

Q. . . . ■ QUEEN'S HILL, which used to be a backwater tucked away behind the station (it's more of a through road now) but contained the main entrance to the old High School. One of the duties of school prefects was to patrol this escape route in pairs during mid-morning break and stop evil-doers slipping off to the pub. I realized I wasn't cut out to be a prefect when I and a much smaller colleague (Deaf Guy and Midget – They Fight Crime!) found several hairy

MY OWN WORST ENEMY

I wake up each day
To invent me again
Through the plots and deceptions
And perceptions of pain
One look in the mirror and what
    do I see?
Burning within
My own worst enemy

I open my mouth
And what will you get?
A friend down the years
Or some bitter old shit
Who can't move a muscle
For the weight of some hurt

That's dimly imagined
And fixing to burst
And cripple the one
Who's brought this on me
And walks in my shoes
My own worst enemy

I deserve better
But he demands more
Shot in the foot
That's nailed to the floor
But there's almost good reason
For this entropy
And I start believing
My own worst enemy

THE NOVA SCOTIA TAR BABY

There was an old white school teacher in the land of Whales, and his boys all called him Sammy. His real name was Arthur Langford. He was stern and reserved and certainly the only person in that school who could remember exactly where this nickname came from. He was named for Sammy Langford, the greatest heavyweight boxer who never won a title.

Nova Scotia looks like a big cannon dangling off the underside of America's eastern seaboard aimed ominously back at New England. Flipper read that in a book called *Halifax, Warden of the North* that had fallen from a manatee viewing platform near the Cape Canaveral launch site. She's a very smart dolphin, but you'd think her areas of scholarly expertise would be a bit patchy to say the least, governed as they are by random acts of gravity. Except they're not patchy – she knows everything!

I don't know how she found out about Sam E. Langford but she did. He had two horrible ring names. First he was The Nova Scotia Tar Baby, and then years later The Boston Tar Baby. His skin was as black as mine is white, and while Flipper says it's OK for her to call me Chalk-ball, or Iceberg, or the Milky Bar Kid, Sam probably didn't care too much for the names he got stuck with.

Sam E. Langford toured the world. Once he posed in front of the Eiffel Tower with a silver-tipped cane and monocle. Living the life with the Dixie Kid; he was pimped-up pugilist royalty. You

thugs waiting at the gate to meet our first truant and narrowly escaped a beating-up. After that it seemed wiser to stay in the Prefects' Room like everyone else, reading *Private Eye* and planning our underground school magazine *Vole*, whose jokes were all uncannily reminiscent of the *Eye* and Monty Python. That led to a lot of trouble too; our first issue triggered three outraged meetings of the school staff. Later it occurred to me that we'd invented the fanzine, years before discovering SF fandom.

On an educational tour of the print works of our local paper the *South Wales Argus*, I cunningly asked a Linotype operator to run off a *Vole: The Underground Magazine* masthead as a demo piece. I still have that slab of metal type, which reads: 'VOLIE: The Underground". This tells you all you need to know about the *South Wales Argus*.

Queen's Hill was also famous in our family for Peter Price's garage (By Appointment to the Langfords). It took Jon's musical expertise to reveal that Joe Strummer from the Clash had lived over the newsagent's on the corner. Joe Who from the What?

R. . . . We were too little to notice that wartime **RATIONING** continued long after World War II was over, but it still cast a shadow in the early 1960s. I remember school dinners – actually lunches – at the Gaer School, and the morning ritual of calling the dinner roster. This made it very clear to the whole class which kids were paying a shilling or so and which charity cases were getting fed for free. One day when I'd somehow lost my dinner money, or maybe spent it on a comic, I learned the hard way that switching to the free list was not an option. God, the embarrassment.

The Gaer canteen food was pretty awful, but we choked it down anyway, even the watery white slime that pretended to be custard. One dark day, though, the sausages were too much. Tough, greasy, horrible – and after an especially

TOO MUCH MUSIC TOO MANY BUILDINGS TOO MANY CARS TOO MANY LANE
EVERYTHING GOES ROUND IN INCREASING CIRCLES BY REMOTE CONTROL FR
MILES AWAY
I LOST MY FOOTING AND I LOST MY WAY
DOWN THE TRAPDOOR DOWN THE DRAIN
POUR ME OUT A COFFEE AT 4 IN THE MORNING
I'VE READ ALL THE SIGNS BUT I DON'T BELIEVE THE WARNINGS
WHAT CAN I SAY?
I'M IN SPLENDID ISOLATION
THROUGH THE WHISPERS & THE SNORING
I WAKE UP & I'M MELTING
FEELING LIKE I'M FALLING
TOO MANY STATIONS AND CORPORATIONS
TOO MANY BILLBOARDS
TOO MANY CHAINS
THE SPICE OF LIFE GROUND DOWN TO ZERO
IT FEELS LIKE SAME STR
U.S.A.
I LOST MY JOB & I LOST MY WAY
DOWN THE TRAPDOOR
REMOTE CONTROL
SAME STREET USA
TRAPDOOR
DOWN THE DRAIN

TRAP DOOR

Too much music
Too many buildings
Too many cars
Too many lanes
Everything goes round in increasing circles
By remote control from miles away
I lost my footing and lost my way
Down the trapdoor, down the drain
Pour me out a coffee at four in the morning
I've read all the signs but I don't believe the warnings
What can I say?
I'm in splendid isolation through the whispers and the snoring
I wake up and I'm melting, I'm feeling like I'm falling
Down the trapdoor, down the drain

Too many stations and corporations
Too many billboards, too many chains
The spice of life down ground to zero
It feels like Same Street USA
I lost my job and I lost my way
Down the trapdoor, down the drain

slow and reluctant meal, one was found abandoned on the floor.

This gave our headmaster a Krazy Kat moment: 'I sense the feel of evil. Every nerve of me vibrates to the symphony of sin. Somewhere, at this moment, crime holds revel.' Outraged, he focused his little grey cells and gathered the suspects in the library. That is, he reconstructed the crime with the same hapless pupils sat around the same canteen table for interrogation. I forget now whether there was a chalked outline of a sausage on the floor.

The questioning was brutal but no one confessed. The mystery remains unsolved to this day. I was glad to have put several feet of alibi between myself and that awful tube of gristle, but still wish I'd managed to lob it further and land it under a different table.

S . . . 'He's that most dangerous of creatures, a clever **SHEEP**.' This famous line from the first-ever episode of *Monty Python's Flying Circus* was clearly inspired by the satanic cunning of South Walian ovines. The sheep is not a creature of the air, but to some baffled investigators it seemed they must be able to levitate. Merthyr Tydfil, you see, was defended in depth by cattle-grids which no hoofed animal could possibly negotiate . . . yet somehow the local sheep made their way into the town centre. Were heavily disguised ewes hitching lifts from unwary motorists? Was it significant that certain planes are called ramjets? Someone call the *Fortean Times*!

Eventually this conundrum was explained by film footage of Merthyr sheep lying down and deftly rolling sideways over the grids. After which they'd rowdily upset dustbins, slash cinema seats and bully old age pensioners until driven off by fierce cries of 'Mint sauce! Mint sauce!' Never underestimate *dafad*, the clever Welsh sheep.

Arthur Machen imagined sheep as one of the animals that murderously rise up against humanity in *The Terror* (1917). After all, 'what would happen to you if a hundred sheep ran after you instead of running from you? There would be no help for it; they would have you down and beat you to death or stifle you.' But Alfred Hitchcock decided to film a rather later author's nightmare of animal revolt, which is why we got *The Birds* rather than *The Sheep*.

I'M STOPPING THIS TRAIN

I'm stopping this train
Let only dead men remain
Rolling on to forever I'm stopping this trai
The way was so clear
But we got stuff in our eyes
Full speed ahead
Crackling through the night
Like a silver bullet
That nobody aimed
That you'll never see coming
Though it's struck with your name

Tearing up the rails
When the fuel is all gone
Getting faster and faster
Rolling on and on and on

I'm stopping this train
Let only dead men remain
Rolling onto forever I'm stopping this trai
Stand up and yell
In the smoke and the flames
I can see in the dark now
I'm stopping this train

I'M STOPPING THIS TRAIN...
LET ONLY DEAD MEN REMAIN
ROLLING ON TO FOREVER
THE WAY WAS SO CLEAR
BUT WE GOT STUFF IN OUR EYES
FULL SPEED AHEAD CRACKLING THROUGH
LIKE A SILVER THE
BULLET NIGHT
THAT
NOBODY
AIMED
THAT
YOU'LL
NEVER
SEE
COMING

THOUGH IT'S STRUCK WITH YOUR NAME
TEARING UP THE RAILS WHEN THE FUEL IS
ALL GONE
GETTING FASTER & FASTER, ROLLING ON &
STAND UP AND YELL IN THE SMOKE AND ON
I CAN SEE IN THE DARK NOW THE FLAMES
I'M STOPPING THIS TRAIN

called him a monster. The great white hopes wouldn't fight him, and even the first black champ, Jack Johnson, refused to give the shorter, tougher man a shot at his title after their prior scrap in 1906. So he pursued Johnson across the country waiting for his chance, just as later, when he was old and blind (in your insular city of the Manhattoes), he'd follow younger boxers around the ring by sound and smell, patiently absorbing the body blows, his long arms and bandaged knuckles feeling for the moment to strike.

There are a lot of black people in Nova Scotia. Flipper says they all talk like jolly whalin' lads in '50s movies. They were Africans who got abducted by aliens and dragged half way across the world to Jamaica. They escaped into the hills and lived free for 50 years. They were called the Maroons. But they were hunted down by the white governor's army and shipped up to the frozen north as punishment.

'You know what the Captain on the spicy rum bottle did after all the pirate mayhem?' asked Flipper.

'I don't know, more mayhem?"

'Exactly, your whiteness, King Charlie Stuart made him Guv'nor of Jamaica, the sugar slave island. There's white sugar, brown sugar, and people dying in the fields. Langford name and Morgan name are from the same place and that's how Sammy got his. Sammy gets the white slaver's name and the quiet white teacher gets the Black maroon fighter's name, and round and round and back and forth it goes in and out of the land of Whales.'

Is that where Whales go to retire?

VERDUN

I don't feel like talking
Or scoring any points
I'm finished now with fighting
I've handed in my gun
I know this thing is over
And I don't really care who won
The grass grows thick and green
All around Verdun

I lied about my age
So I could volunteer
It didn't feel like nothing
Ooooh, small beer
Now I'm on a bus from the hospital
Patched up and well fed
In a badly cut suit
With a bandage round my head

I came straight out of shock
Back onto the shopfloor
It hurts my eyes to work
I can't seem to get things done
There's something in between me
And everything before
I still taste the earth
All around Verdun

Hoppy's gone forever
Billy's gone for good
But part of me came back again
I always knew it would
A snapshot and a postcard
That fell into the sun
The grass grows thick and green
All around Verdun

One of the mysteries of South Wales is why Newport isn't a World Heritage site with tourists flocking in tens of thousands to see and ride on the amazing **TRANSPORTER BRIDGE** across the Usk. Its trademark towers – like giant electricity pylons – and the long high span between them are the first clear sign of Newport you see from the train. Welcome home.

When we were innocent tots with no access to Google, we had no idea that this was such a rare and special kind of bridge. All the same, it was a thrill to be carried very slowly over the river's filthy grey water and mud on a moving platform ('gondola' is the technical term) controlled from a small pointy-roofed house in one corner. With a maximum of six cars and a hundred and something pedestrians in each load, it definitely wasn't built for the age of the M4 motorway.

Nothing special seems to have happened on the Transporter Bridge centenary in 2006*, though it was all lit up with fireworks for the eve of the millennium. The most exciting moment came when it was hijacked during the 1984-1985 miners' strike. 'Transport this bridge to Cuba, or Margaret Thatcher gets it!' Well, not quite: some mining pickets occupied the control house on 30 August 1984 and halted the gondola in midstream – right over the Usk's deep-water channel so as to block shipping. Letting ships through is, of course, the reason for having such a peculiar bridge design in the first place.

Although the militant miners had stocked up for a two-week siege, the police defeated them that same night by use of satanic cunning. After waiting for most of the shore pickets to get bored and go home, Chief Superintendent Fred Wye had his men storm the engine room under the bridge's east tower. A few quiet arrests later, they overrode the platform control-house and brought the gondola home again like a dog on a long lead. Less spectacular than having the SAS abseil from the top span with a shower of stun grenades, but probably easier on everybody's nerves.

URBAN LEGENDS. There is an irrational belief among visitors to Wales that laver bread is a food. It is, in fact, seaweed. Researchers have come to suspect that offering this dank green substance as gourmet nosh is a practical joke played

*Actually, there was a huge two-day music festival in Victoria Park on the east side of the bridge, organized by Richard King (John Cale's nephew). Someone told him I had a song that mentioned the Transporter Bridge, so I got to play the Skull Orchard tunes with Julian, Cousin Mark, Mark Davenport, Matt and Carlton – and then to close the show with the hastily reassembled Three Johns, who were always quite popular in the 'Port. Despite the best efforts of some local councilors to ruin it, the Festival was hugely successful, a proper multicultural celebration. The next day, we got to climb to the top of that massive old bridge and act like tourists in our own town.—JL

by the Welsh on unsuspecting tourists. A bit like the famous Arab prank of pretending that the tastiest part of a sheep is the eyeball. ('He believed it, Abdul! He *believed* it!")

It is widely believed in Chicago that the national dish of South Wales is macaroni cheese, baked in the oven with bacon and sausages. Our Mum loves to make it (very good, too) and Jon's lads Jimmy and Tommy expect it as part of traditional Welsh cuisine whenever they're in Newport.

It is not so widely believed that our Grandmother Len was a barmaid at the Upper Cock pub in Croesyceiliog during the Chartist Riots. But give on a bit longer to spread this highly plausible legend and it may yet get into the history books.

The many stories about Welshmen, sheep and wellies will not be discussed in this scholarly text, for fear that our mother might read it. The Welsh were linked with certain activities as long ago as the sixteenth century, as shown by a notorious piece of English legislation: 'An Acte for the contynuyng of the Statutes for Beggars and Vacabundes; and ayenst conveyaunce of Horses and Mares out of this realme; ayenst Wellsshemen making affraies in the Countyes of Hereford Gloucestre and Salop; and ayenst the vice of Buggery' (18 Hen. 8, c. 6, 1536). Fortunately for all concerned, this act was repealed in 1863.

V . . . ■

Exotic food was in short supply in 1960s Newport. There was a lone Indian restaurant somewhere beyond the shady end of Commercial Street, but it was regarded with a certain superstitious dread. The tandoori oven hadn't been invented (all right, imported) and Newportonians didn't even know what chicken tikka masala *was*.

But in our cosmopolitan way we regularly dined on **VESTA** Beef Curry, a dark brown sludge reconstituted from a rattly packet of dried lumps. The measured portion of very white, fibre-free rice was in another packet. *Just Add Water!* Dad would pep up this grim ready-meal with fancy side dishes of chopped onion (yum), banana (yum) and tomato (ugh, but that's just me). Even today, a nibble of raw onion still conjures up the whole scene, though not at the excruciating length achieved by Proust's magic biscuit. It all feels part of such a remote past that I was stunned to find that Vesta Beef Curry is still on sale. Perhaps they've changed the formula. I certainly hope so.

ON NOVEMBER 4TH 1839 MORE THAN TWENTY SUPPORTERS OF THE CHARTIST MOVEMENT, WHICH SOUGHT TO ESTABLISH DEMOCRATIC RIGHTS FOR ALL MEN, DIED IN AN EXCHANGE OF SHOTS AT THE WESTGATE HOTEL NEWPORT. TEN WERE BURIED IN THIS CHURCHYARD IN UNMARKED GRAVES. THIS STONE IS DEDICATED TO THEIR MEMORY.

NATIONAL CHARTER ASSOCIATION OF GREAT BRITAIN

THIS IS OUR CHARTER.
UNIVERSAL SUFFRAGE.
VOTE BY BALLOT.
ANNUAL PARLIAMENTS.
Equal Electoral Districts.
PAYMENT OF MEMBERS.
NO PROPERTY QUALIFICATION.

TRUTH IS OUR GUIDE.

" The Male Adult Population of the British Empire is SEVEN MILLIONS, of which EIGHT HUNDRED THOUSAND *only* are Enfranchised!"

Name_____ No. *15016*

Date of Entry_____

PRESIDENT ...... PHILIP McGRATH.
TREASURER ...... FEARGUS O'CONNOR.
SECRETARY ...... THOMAS M. WHEELER.

Steurter, Printer, Bethnal Green, London.

HUNTED

I hunt and I'm hunted, but I never got taken up topside. I've got nicks in my fins from Orca teeth, a squid-scarred barnacled back full of harpoons and I'm happy to crunch the odd whaling boat betwixt my jaws if needs be. I'm a mammal (airy and hairy) so I have to breach once in a while, but when necessary I can hold my breath for hours. There was no boat strong enough, no net big enough, to get me up there.

Flipper told me how she got abducted by aliens a long time ago as well. 'They caught me up in a net with a load of loose fish. Took me in the dry and give me the fin ring. Said I'm always on their radar from here on inwards; under, over and through. Knowing every last thing, always.'

ON THE NATURE OF HIRAETH

Far away a voice is calling, bells of memory chime, come home again, come home again, it calls through the oceans of time.
The silt-choked waters of the Severn estuary lie brown and flat for miles around me. They lap weakly at my vastness. But above the steep fossil cliffs I see the pleasant blue whale-shaped hills of Gwent tumbling off over the horizon, keeping their welcome and waiting patiently to kiss away two hundred years of hiraeth.
Whales, Whales, bloody great fishes are whales!
The lilting cadences of a 50-piece whale voice choir drift down from the valleys, through clouds and rain, resonating up (in delightful 4-part harmony) from the deep tunnels and shafts you yourselves cut through black earth, rock and

ancient layers of dry bone sediment, from the hillsides with the little crosses where you choked your children on slag, so the orange lamps can light the night. Dead families from ancient oceans are calling me.

We'll kiss away each hour of hiraeth . . .
I'm huge and white and I'm burning up. I'm like a fat bloke sunbathing with his shirt off on a bank holiday Monday. Yes, finally I'm a beached whale – or what did Flipper call me that one time in the Florida Strait: a bleached whale?

Can I just say I'm bloody sick of you lot standing round staring at me with your cameras and lights and your funny furry microphones, (what sort of thieving dinosaur-egg sucking mammal did you make that from anyway?) This tide sucks, but I'm not budging. You can all see that I've lived too long, and now it's almost done. Just make sure you smile when you call me a mythical monster.

When you come home again . . .
Hiraeth is a word that has no direction equivalent in English (or Dolphin), but we whales understand it perfectly. How could we not? It's our sextant, our compass, our GPS and just one more reason I'm stuck here helpless in these shifting shallows. So what does hiraeth mean again? It implies a longing, a yearning, a primitive and almost sexual ache for home, and yes, I was almost there.

Tubby Brothers

SOMEONE'S DEAD IN BLEWITT STREET
DOWN THE STAIRS WE CRIPPED SOME PAINT
DECLINED SWEET SHERRY, HAD SOME TEA
AND HOVERED SILENTLY

I REMEMBER ABERFAN
ROWS OF LITTLE CROSSES UP ON THE HILL
WOULDN'T SWIM IN THE CHANNEL THOUGH
PEOPLE PARALYSED AT OXWICH BAY
2 CONTAINERS FULL
OF CHEMICALS
CAN'T TAKE THE BOY DOWN THERE
WHAT WOULD
HIS MOTHER
SAY?

SOMEONE'S DEAD IN CALDICOT
DIG THEIR GRAVE IN A BRAND NEW PLOT

THEY DUG THEIR GRAVE IN A BRAND NEW PLOT
SEE THE FOOTBRIDGE HAS BEEN TAKEN DOWN
IT ONLY TAKES FIVE MINUTES TO DRIVE THROUGH TOWN
BUT THE FLOWERS LOOK LIKE WOUNDS
THE ROADS CUT DEEP & DIRECT, THE RAILWAYS CHANGE
THEIR NAMES & DON'T CONNECT

SOMEONE'S DEAD
IN CLARENCE PLACE
A DRY PALMED
HANDSHAKE
& A FACE LIKE A
WELL KEPT GRAVE
THERE'S SOME PROBLEM
WITH THE FEET
BUT WE WERE
SOFT SPOKEN, FORMAL
& DISCREET

WHEN THE LID IS DOWN
AND YOU'RE UNDERGROUND
WE WAIT AND WATCH
JUST HANGING 'ROUND AND DREAM OF HORSES IN BLACK FEATHERS
BREATHING HEAVY AT THE
FRONT OF THE
MOTORCADE

TUBBY BROTHERS

Someone's dead in Blewitt Street
Down the stairs we chipped some paint
Declined sweet sherry, had some tea
And hovered silently.

Someone's dead in Caldicot
They dug their grave on a brand new plot
See the footbridge has been taken down
It only takes five minutes drive through
    town
But the flowers look like wounds
And the roads cut deep and direct
The railways change their names and
    don't connect

I remember Aberfan
Rows of little crosses upon the hill
I wouldn't swim in the channel though
    now
People paralyzed at Oxwich Bay
Two containers full of chemicals
Can't take the boy down there,
what would his mother say?

Someone's dead in Clarence Place
A dry palmed handshake and a face like a
    well kept grave
There was some problem with the feet
But we were soft spoken, formal and
    discrete
When the lid is down and you're
    underground
We wait and watch hanging around
And dream of horses in black feathers
Breathing heavy at the front of the
    motorcade

W . . . . I've got an O-level in **WOODWORK**, I'll have you know, although I was and am terrible at actually making things. Grown men have wept at the sight of a Langford mortice and tenon joint. Here the rectangular tongue of wood is supposed to fit so snugly into the matching slot that you hardly need glue. In my rough hands, the result was always a obscene wooden lump that wobbled around in a kind of splintery crater. Much furtive packing with cardboard was needed, and sometimes help from forbidden nails or screws.

I must have got through the O-level exam by remembering the theory. Smell-free sycamore is the wood for kitchen use. Lignum vitae is ever so dense, while balsa wood isn't. Elm is what you use for coffins: impossible to forget because there was a boy called Elms in our class and Mr Golledge the woodwork master never mentioned his name without growling, 'Elms . . . *coffin wood.*' Perhaps Elms hated this as much as I hated the way Golledge insisted on calling me Sammy. He'd been taught maths by Dad's father, Arthur Langford, whose pupils in the 1950s called him after the well-known black boxer Sammy Langford. Thanks to the humorous Mr Golledge, I was lumbered with the same nickname for the rest of my Newport High School days. No, I'm still not in a forgiving mood.

When high crimes were committed in the workshop – things like bodging a loose mortice-and-tenon with cardboard, or defiantly not answering to 'Sammy' – the Golledge Kangaroo Court would administer terrifying justice. He'd select a sheet of wood from the offcuts box and slowly, menacingly, use the electric bandsaw to cut out a shape like a double-width cricket bat. The accused had to bend over and take a mighty thwack on the buttocks from this terror weapon. If it broke, the ordeal by woodwork was over. If not, it proved you were a witch and deserved another whack. Probably there's a law against that kind of thing now.

X . . . . is for **BIDDEN**. Because there is no X in the Welsh alphabet, our bilingual signs carefully explain for the benefit of Welsh monoglots that *Taxis* are in fact *Tacsis* and – far up in the frozen north – *Wrexham* is *Wrecsam*. Otherwise everyone would be terribly confused. Keep an eye out in the supermarket for the famous South Walian triple-CS brandy.

Other difficult Welsh words include the double-decker *bws*, the seaside *promenad*, the eighteen-hole *cwrs golff*, and (for indoor games) the *clwb snŵcer*. If tourists want to go native and take a leek, they should use the *toiledau* – being careful not to confuse this amenity with the *teledu* or television. No one is quite sure why, when a word for TV had to be reluctantly added to the Welsh language, they chose one whose English dictionary definition is 'the stinking badger of Java".

Y . . ■ One, or maybe more than one, of our long-ago family outings was to Symonds **YAT** in Herefordshire, which is essentially a large lump of rock covered in trees standing next to the River Wye. The guidebooks credit it with great natural beauty (as distinct from the Cwmbran valley's trademark hill Twmbarlwm, which is more famous for great natural deformity: it shows on the skyline with a large off-centre pimple near the top).

There was something disappointing about this Yat expedition. Perhaps we picked a day when the touristy bits were closed: at least, I can't remember a single detail of the famous hand-powered rope ferry or the famous maze. The real problem may have been that I was young enough to expect great things, and thought Symonds Yat would be an exotic animal named for its inventor, like Thompson's Gazelle or Bosman's Potto. It would be something partway between yeti and yak, and would live at the heart of the maze. But I never got to see it.

Z . . ■ The **ZAMPOGNA**, as we all know, is the Italian bagpipe. This is relevant to any reminiscences of South Wales because, in the first place, the region has a largish Italian community which I've shockingly failed to mention until now. They live mostly on zabaglione, ziti, zucchini and Heinz Tomato Zuppe. In the second place, the zampogna is one of the few instruments brother Jon has never played with his famous *zoppo* (Italian for syncopation). Our family is deeply thankful for this. ∗

∗ Please note the enormous restraint with which I avoided dragging in the *zufolo*, 'a small flute or flageolet used for training singing birds.' We trained our budgie Joey on cuttlefish, but he never developed any talent, or tentacles (see Arthur Machen).

I AM THE LAW

Can't you see
You're going to spend your life with me
Yes it's true
I'm going to twist and bend on you
Don't you understand?
I am the law and you are a man
Everyday
Just out of sight not too far away
Every week
Talking a language you can't speak
Every year
Beat with a mallet in a poor man's ear
This money pump of power knows
The best defense is attack
But how can you climb back on the tracks
With the law riding on your back
There's the crack
Heads will bow and legs will snap
Right down through history
It's one for you and a hundred for me
Don't you understand?

I AM THE LAW!
CAN'T YOU SEE? YOU'RE GONNA SPEND YOUR LIFE WITH ME YES ITS TRUE I'M GOING TO TWIST & BEND ON YOU DON'T YOU UNDERSTAND? I AM THE LAW & YOU ARE A MAN
THAT MONEY PUMP OF POWER KNOWS THE BEST DEFENCE IS ATTACK
EVERYDAY JUST OUT OF SIGHT NOT TOO FAR AWAY
BUT HOW CAN YOU MOVE BACK ON THE TRACK WITH THE LAW RIDING ON YOUR BACK
EVERY WEEK TALKING IN A LANGUAGE YOU CAN'T SPEAK EVERY YEAR BEAT WITH A MALLET IN A POOR MAN'S EAR
HERE'S THE CRACK HEADS WILL BOW AND LEGS WILL SNAP RIGHT DOWN THROUGH HISTORY IT'S ONE FOR YOU & 100 FOR ME DON'T YOU UNDERSTAND?

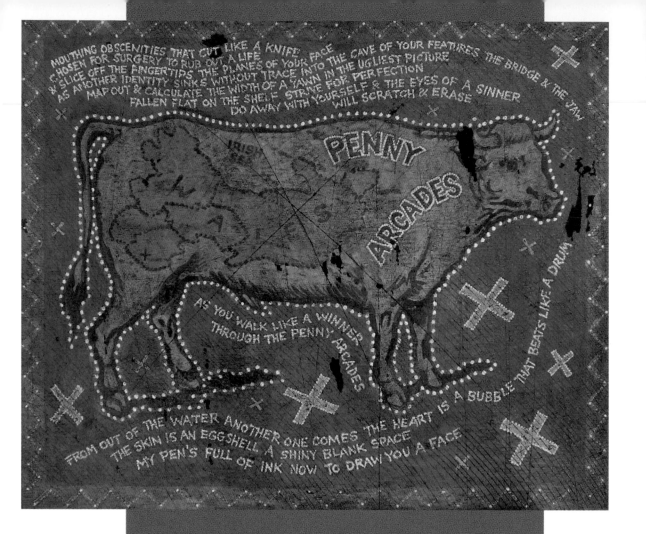

PENNY ARCADES

Mouthing obscenities that cut like a knife
That's chosen for surgery, to rub out a life
And slice off the finger-tips, the planes of our face
As another identity sinks without trace
Into the cave of your features, the bridge and the jaw
You map out and calculate the width of a yawn
As the ugliest picture falls flat on the shelf
Strive for perfection, do away with yourself
And the eyes of a sinner will scratch and erase
As you walk like a winner through the penny arcades
From out of the water another one comes
The heart is a bubble that beats like a drum
The skin is an eggshell, a shiny blank space
This pen's full of ink now, to draw you a face

FLIPPER R.I.P.

Whale meat again, don't know where don't know when . . .

She never really recovered from the loss of her library. I mean that metaphorically; it would be insane for a marine mammal to keep a huge pile of books underwater. They'd go all mulchy and the sea worms would have a feast. The little coral grotto of alphabetized shelving I picture was in her head, and when it finally evaporated she was devastated. I could tell her sonar wasn't working anymore. Her navigational skills became non-existent and when she said she could take me to the Land Of Whales, I got a sinking feeling in my blowholes. We hadn't been on a trip like that since 1954.

She was a total spy-hopper; always poking her head above the surface to look around. The other dolphins couldn't care less about your dry land; they're still mad at the insects. But Flipper, as you know, was always obsessed with facts and figures and gathering information. She seemed to suck it in through the air-waves. But in the end it was two-way traffic.

Flipper saw my whiteness as proof of moral purity. She was also convinced I was a virgin. 'Hey, Coke-spoon, you never have a nice mating in a long while? You should find a big girl like Pearl!' she clicked with glee back in Scammon's lagoon. Who the hell is Pearl? I enquired. 'Mr. Crabs' baby, I saw her in my head, remember? She'll give you some playful rubbing to stimulate your hormones and no worries!' Too much information . . .

Towards the end of our last long journey I was munching a mud hole by the edge of the European continental shelf and when I looked around she was gone. I peered deep into the abyss but I never saw her again.

TWENTY QUESTIONS

What or who am I? Am I alive or dead? Am I fictional? Did I have my own TV show in the sixties? No, I'm not Tom Jones, (or Flipper). I'm not a creature, I'm a concept. Am I bigger than a loaf of white sliced bread? No, I'm not Aer Lingus! Do you know me? That's a tough question because you think you know everything. No, I'm not the whale that swallowed Jonah. We're not even related. Bloody biblical hitchhiker, spat out on some faraway beach, he should have been grateful. And for your information, there is no God and very soon there won't be any mysteries. That's another no! Am I turbulence? Like when you're cocooned in some tiny commuter jet thousands of feet over West Texas being buffeted violently by pockets of warm wet air and I give you a little glimpse of the horror and scale of it all, but you just slide your nose into some magazine from the seat pocket in front of you and ignore me? Am I a big white cloud? You're getting warmer. Am I garden gnome syndrome? Am I holding back the chaos beyond the edge of your vision, while the earth coughs and sneezes in ever more desperate attempts to shake you off? Can you burn me? Am I a fuel? Yes, you're very warm. Am I coal? You're burning hot but you'd better shut your bloody mouths when you're talking to me! Is that a heron? My hump is huge, my brow is wrinkled. I am quite alone. Do you smell land where there is no land? Who painted the signposts green? Was I confused, did I misread the information provided? How do I get to the country of Whales?

MESSAGE IN A BOTTLE
Ahab's crew watched and waited for the chick inside him to hatch, like he was a big egg, a big dinosaur's egg. Wait 'til you cut me open tomorrow and read the messages I've been carrying inside me and see the broken beaks and armor of monstrous new predators you have never imagined littered through the tunnels of my gut. You'll never know the half of it.

THE DEATH OF MOBY DICK
In one early version of the book I am the only survivor, the bit about Ishmael and the savage's coffin got lost at the printers and, despite the first-person narrative, I am the only one who doesn't die. Imagine that! Now you can write a song about me and call it *The Death of Moby Dick,* and though the hunt is over and the monsters have finally won, it'll be the last thing ever to cross your lips, because now I'm just like you. There's really no difference at all.

Where ever you wander
Where ever you'll be
Up there in the Rhondda
Down here by the sea
We're calling you home, calling you home
And this time it's to stay
And I, I can fly . . .

SOLOMON JONES

There's a face on the wall
Of this fine institution
A face from the past
Looking into the future
Where the truth often hurts
But it's somewhere it's needed
He dipped his foot in the water
But the water kept moving
So nothing can be the same
It's just who we blame
I get to work in the mine
You get to do what you like

The current flows one way
I'm leaving Garndiffaith today
The power flows one way
I'm going away

No, Daddy's not mad
He just used to be lazy
We were walking to Newport
Then the boys all went crazy
Don't know how many died
Or just crawled off to hide
On the Devil's Heap of Stones
They cornered Solomon Jones

The current flows one way
We're leaving the valleys today
Leaving the old world
Transported away

Where the daffodils grow
In the hills of Tasmania
This swimming on dry land
Is still part of our nature
Sending mail on the sea
I hope you're there to receive it
We always promised the world
And hoped the world would believe it

The winds blowing our way
We're leaving Australia today
The power flows one way
We're leaving today
Now I'm a face at a window
Staring out at the Pennines
Put all my money in textiles
& I died as an exile
And all the owners and slaves
Are disguised but not changed
Sometimes you get what you ask for
It's time to start asking for more

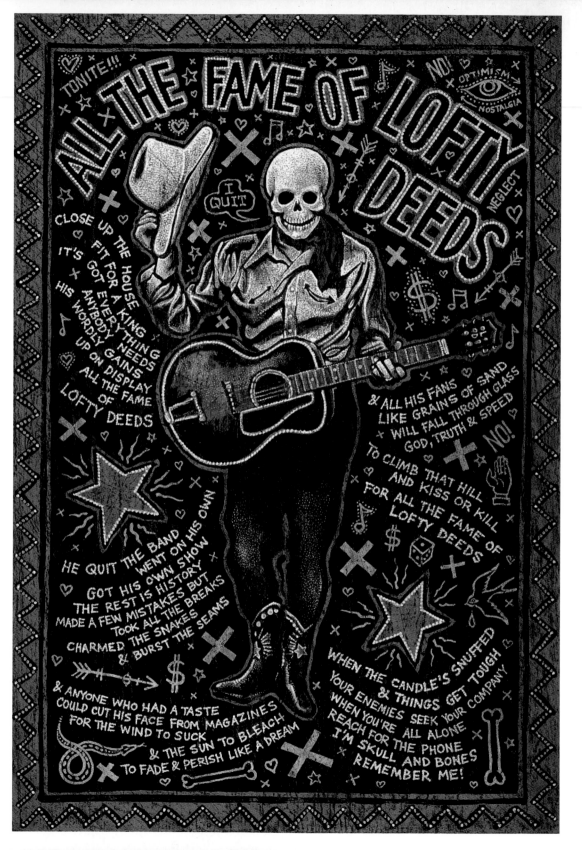

INDEX OF ART

DENIS LANGFORD'S PHOTOGRAPHS

Den loved to take pictures. There are still boxes and boxes of slides, stretching back to the early sixties, in a cupboard in our Mum's bedroom. He didn't like taking pictures of people much (he preferred Alps and cliffs), but sometimes, when he had a little film left to use up at the end of a roll, he'd turn the camera on us or the dogs – or, rarer still, on the town we lived in.

Thanks to Jack Salter for scanning in the images reproduced here.

ACKNOWLEDGMENTS

Thanks to Helen, Jimmy & Tommy, Hazel, Johnny Sicolo for the grog, Ron & Wendy Weiss, the Billions Corporation, Mekons & their deputies, Doug & Chris Garofalo, Jack Salter, Mark & Leslie & the boys, Bloodshot Records, everyone at HSB, Arthur & Lenny Pearse, 3 Johns, the Hideout, Sally Timms, Wacos, Mark & Nancy, Colleen & Mike Miller, the Old Town School of Folk Music, Yard Dog, Louise & Dave Talbott, John Peel, Vickie & Becky, Billy Bones, the Welcome Home, Patti Vega, Rico & Mindy, the Stowaway, Steve & Katherine at VCP, Brett Oaten, Jim Elkington, the Engineers, Maldwyn & the history committee, John Rice, Kathy Acker, the Murenger, Sassy Hicks, Ralph & the Ponytails, Helmi Coyne & Robert & Eugene, Peter Wright at Low Noise Music, Amy Lombardi, the Angel, Val & John Richards, the Tsatsos & Lekousis, the Exchange, Titch Jones, FitzGerald's, CBM, the Carpenters Arms, Bob & Alice, 2 Marks & a Frank, the Chartists, Barry & Julie & Chelsea, Janet at Barnabas, the Ivy Bush, Renee White, the Legendary Horseshoe Tavern, Marty & Connie, the Gaer Inn, Roger Knox, Tawny Newsome, TJs, House Theater, Stow Hill Labour Club, ICADP, the Riverside, Alan Storey, Kengineer, Walkabout Theater, Jean Cook, the Critter, the Upper Cocks, Cynthia P., Bonnie Prince Billy, Newport County, Sean Dundon, Mike & LUSC America, Guto, Norm & Marty & everyone at XRT, Greil & Jenny, Delilah's, $1000 Car, Denise & Christy at LeMieux, Tony Baker, the Parc-Y-Prior, Thaddeus, Joe Camarillo & Kim, Marc Riley, the Dock Social Club, Brian Joseph, Tootsies Orchid Lounge, Mrs. Mac, the Six In Hand, Ray & the Levitation Choir, Jon & Jen Rauhouse, Bet Jones, the Handpost, Edith Frost, Grove Park Rangers, Ryan Hembrey, Peter Doyle, the Six Bells, Johnny Cash, Theresa James at White Wings Press, the Sexy, Joe Strummer, the Bull Inn, Sarah Vowell, Diverse, Wouter at Galerie Link, the Ship & Pilot, the Far Forlorn, Discount Chiefs, Lester Bangs, Dublin Moran, Jonathan Franzen, the Ship, FMC, Terry Nelson, David Ravel, Brews, Jane & Tim in Paddo, ATC, the Ex, Tony & Miry & Leo, TAG, Lyceum Tavern, Chumbas, Vito Acconci, Dan Massey, the Baron, Chris Mills, Dogfish Head, the Cross Keys, the MAN band, Friendly Tap, Gary & Keith, Yellowhammers, the Dirty Duck, Clinton Walker, Ken & Lynn, the Borderers, Alex & Edie, the Metro, Hatch Showprint, Patrick Eyres & New Arcadia Press, Tony Fitzpatrick, Bonerama, Unca Dave, Stuart Coupe, Handsome Family, Nev & Sue, Jane Baxter-Miller, U-Roy, the Crow's Nest, Alex & Kat, the Merry Miller, David Hando, Schuba's, Jean & John Timms, the Castell-Y-Bwch, Sadies & Goods, the Hanbury Arms, Chuck Kouri, the Rowlands & the Jolliffes, Jon Kardon, Alejandro Escovedo, Mark Guarino, Garndiffaith RFC, Damaged Goods in Seattle, the Ochoas, Tom & Lynne, the Waterloo, Phillip Bither, Swells & Kathryn, the Dolphin, Thomas Masters, Le Pub, Fargo in Paris, Mighty Tea Cossack, the Greenhouse, Dave Alvin, the Westgate Hotel, the Evans & the Cobbetts, LL, Touch & Go, Rosie Flores, the Llewellyns, the Commercial, Dick Gaughan, Spillers, the Trout Vaults, Paul Flynn MP, TJ Clark, Jean & Ken Cromwell, GLC, the Wheatsheaf, Julian & Anne, the Friday night gang, Jo & Katryn, the Greyhound, Charlotte & John, Yow, Luc Sante, the Cambrian Arms, Anne Lehman, Cheap, Sweaty Fun, Man is Man, the Lamb, Nobby & his website, Michel in Zurich & Diana & Johanna, the Gate, Brenda & Glen & Cora, the Good Fork, Exleys & Pecha Kucha, the King Billy, Majorie & Irvine Young, the Faversham Hotel, D.O.Cornelius, Super-Normals, Big Kev, Laura Thoms, the Talisman, Jason Walker, the Fenton, Peter Taub & Yolanda, the Lahore, Pete & Debbie, the Three Horseshoes, Elvis Costello, Da Vinci's, Lincoln at McCabe's, Sheila Sachs, the Ridgeway, Panto crew, Kerry in Calgary, Boocock, Jon Styler, Bar Amber, Frank & Liane, 3 Floyds, Finbar Donnelly, the Galaxy, Hogan, Newport Sub-Aqua Club, Piers & Brendan & Paul, the Burches, Terry Atkinson, Gang of Four, the Tredegar Arms, Friends of the Newport Transporter Bridge, Mr & Mrs Smokey, the Hornblower, Give Me Memphis, Mr. Ash, the Potters, Carlos at the Crafty Beaver on Lawrence, the Albert, Paul & Gill down the Gower, the Prince of Wales Pub, Newport Market, the Three Blackbirds, ROIR, the Black Lion, Chrissie Wilson, that pub by the bus station with the bald parrot, Tesoros, the Taff Vale, Joe Angio, Cafe du Nord, the King's Head, Rogue Buddha, Wendy Frith, Dr. Who & all the other exiles . . .

CHOIR AND CREW AT HSB FESTIVAL IN GOLDEN GATE PARK, SAN FRANCISCO, 2008

THE BURLINGTON WELSH MALE CHORUS

The first band I ever produced was Ralph and the Ponytails. Bob Last from Fast Product had seen them opening for the Rezillos; he said they were from Newport, like me, though I'd never heard of them. At this point I'd played drums on one Mekons 45 (not even recorded in a proper studio), but I became the obvious choice to sprinkle fairy dust on 'James Bond,' the Ponytails' debut release. There were nine of them (I think), led by Michael 'Ralph' Mulcahy, a wild Irish Catholic boy from the Bettws estate who was about to move up to Leeds. We became hostile roommates in various cramped flats and bedsits. He was not an easy man to be around but he was generally worth the trouble. I remember seeing him perched on Robert Wyatt's lap backstage at a Scritti Politti gig at the Electric Ballroom in Camden the night the single arrived. Someone had screwed up and 'James Bond' ended up on both sides of the record. They'd gone on stage in full Newport County kit half an hour before the doors opened, with me and Vicky Aspinall from the Raincoats donning tangerine shirts to make up the eleven.

Ralph was a heroic but flawed leader; the other Ponytails were firemen, nurses, astronauts and sheep farmers, and one of them was called Julian 'Juice' Murray. He left Wales for Toronto in the 1980s and joined a male voice choir just like the ones they have in every village up the valleys back home. He sent me a postcard from Grand Cayman telling me all about it. They were called the Burlington Welsh Male Chorus and they were on tour in Grand Cayman!

When the Sadies were recording their double live album at Lee's in Toronto a few years back, I went for a drink with Julian and some of the choirboys. He'd just been appointed to their all powerful committee and had decided it was time to shake things up. I mentioned *Back into the Future*, a semi-live album by Man, my favorite Welsh space rockers, released back in 1973. They used a male voice choir on a song called 'C'Mon,' which had an epic meandering instrumental section that I love to this day. We pondered a project in which we could utilize the choir and came up with the idea of a touring musical called *The Death of Moby Dick*, with the

PRESIDENT JULIAN OF NEWPORT

Burlingtons, the Sadies, and the Good Brothers as the Pequod's crew – and me as the whale. There would be sea shanties, blood, blubber, beer, banjoes, and punk rock. This was just the beer talking, though I did end up writing a peculiar short story as a result (see elsewhere in this book), but the prospect of taking on an even larger and more cumbersome outfit than the Mekons appealed to my well-nurtured masochistic streak and I asked the choir to come and sing with me at CeltFest 2007 in Chicago's Grant Park. Fortunately, Mayor Daley was picking up the tab.

The tunes on the original *Skull Orchard* album were unknowingly written with a Welsh male voice choir in mind. Some might indeed be described as epic. They were meant to be sung at international rugby matches in an alternative universe where Tom Jones is the president of a free Welsh republic and Garndiffaith win the Heineken Cup. As soon as we started rehearsing at the

DAVE NAGLER

Hideout, it became apparent that the songs would have to be re-recorded with these boys onboard. (I keep calling them boys, but they're not – they are mature men, some even more mature than me.)

We recorded their parts up in Toronto, with Paul Aucoin (aka the Critter) engineering. Dave Nagler wrote phenomenal arrangements and was unafraid to stand for hours in the studio beating a performance out of the choir. It was hot and smelly in there, and we didn't have a lot of time, but the high ceilings and hard surfaces produced

the awesome noise we needed and – like everything with the Burlington Welsh Male Chorus – it soon turned into a party.

They move as a pack. They have a fierce collective thirst and a wit to equal it. Last time they came to town, I got a text message requesting eight bottles of whiskey – any kind, as long as the name began with Glen. The *San Francisco Chronicle* described their locust-like beer consumption at the 2008 Hardly Strictly Bluegrass Festival with chilling accuracy. Many of them remind me of my old uncles back in Wales. That is not necessarily a good thing. I took my mother to see me play with them in Welles Park at the Folk & Roots Festival. 'Where you from, love?' asks one of the boys. 'Newport,' she replies. 'Oh, I am sorry,' he says with eyes full of sympathy. Later they put her in a chair on the stage at Ginger's Alehouse and gave her a private performance of 'The Wonder of You.' The men of the choir are stout and gray, and some would say I fit in with them rather too well.

That's because they're mostly expats like me – romantic and economic exiles from grim post-'60s Britain, merchant seaman, rugby players, drinkers, a Cornishman and even a Yorkshireman – the ones that got away. Outside the Hideout after our first rehearsal, my wife Helen pulled up in the van and our youngest boy Tommy pointed into the throng and yelled 'There's Daddy! No, there's Daddy! No, *there's* Daddy!'

ALAN DOUGHTY (TIM BREW)

MARC DURANTE (MARTY PEREZ)

STEVE GOULDING

JONNY ELVIS (CASEY ORR)

COURAGE WALES

SHIP **AND** PILOT

Traditional Bar Games   Local Community Pub

BAR

celtic fest

RECORDING INFORMATION

Original *Skull Orchard* recordings by Ken Sluiter and Mike Hagler at Kingsize Sound Laboratories, Chicago, August 1997.

JON LANGFORD – vocals, guitar etc. **ALAN DOUGHTY** – bass and vocals. **MARC DURANTE** – Fender 6-string guitar, Rickenbacker 12-string guitar, and 1953 Maccaferri plastic guitar. **STEVE GOULDING** – drumkit and vocals.

JOHN RICE – fiddle on 'Youghal,' 'Pill Sailor,' 'Inside the Whale' and 'Tom Jones Levitation.' **EDITH FROST** - vocals on 'Penny Arcades,' 'Verdun' and 'Tom Jones Levitation.' **SALLY TIMMS** – narration on 'Tom Jones Levitation.' **JANE BAXTER-MILLER** – vocals on 'Youghal.' **JOHN HYATT** and **LU EDMONDS** - vocals on 'Penny Arcades.' **FRED ARMISEN** – percussion on 'Last Count.' **TRACEY DEAR** – Mandolin on 'Sentimental Marching Song.' **TOM RAY** – ukulele on 'Sentimental Marching Song,' 'My Own Worst Enemy,' 'I'm Stopping This Train' and 'Deep Sea Diver.' **MARK & ZACK PRICE** – transatlantic talk on 'Deep Sea Diver.' **RICO BELL** – accordion on 'Pill Sailor.' **PAUL MERTENS** and **WALLY MA** – Brass on 'Sentimental Marching Song' and 'I'm Stopping This Train.' **PAUL MERTENS** – alto flute on 'My Own Worst Enemy,' baritone sax on 'Deep Sea Diver.' **DEAN SCHLABOWSKE** – vocals on 'Deep Sea Diver.' Excerpt from 'The Taff' (track 14) performed by **CARLTON B. MORGAN**. **JULIAN HAYMAN** – Inter-valley exploration.

THE BURLINGTON WELSH MALE CHORUS recorded at Hallah Toronto, April 2008, by Paul Aucoin.

BARKLEY MCKAY – piano and organ on 'Green Valleys' and 'Verdun,' recorded at Leeds Music College. **JOHN RICE** – wah-wah guitar on 'Verdun' recorded at Phlosswerx. Other overdubs recorded at Northbranch with Ryan Neuschafer.

Skull Orchard Revisited mixed by Ian Caple at The Barn in Sussex, January 2010.

'Tubby Brothers,' 'I Am the Law,' 'My Own Worst Enemy,' and 'I'm Stopping This Train' mixed by Ken Sluiter, Alhambra, Calif., 2008.

Mastered by Blaise Barton, November 2010

Members of the **BURLINGTON WELSH MALE CHORUS** performing on this recording are: Cye Beechey, Keith Bryan, Robert Buckberrough, John Burrough, Bob Cunningham, Jim Doran, Larry Doyle, John Edwards, Richard Harvey, Sid Hibberd, David Hindley, Craig Howells, Gerry Hubball, Barry Hyslop, Hugh Johnson, Huw Jones, Dennis Kerr, Simon Lewis, Barrie Llewellyn, Bill Mann, John McMillan, Andy Morgan, Julian Murray, Tony Murray, David Paul, Bill Richards, Donny Shaw, Mike Skyrme, Nigel Thorne, Archie Waddell, Johnny Walker, Gerry Welham, George Wentworth, Adrian Williams, Bob Williams, David Williams, Gareth Williams, Ray Williams, John Woolley, Martin Zimber. Their performance is dedicated to the memory of Gerry Hubball ('gone but never forgotten').

Choir arrangements by David Nagler. Thanks to Jean Cook, Craig Howells (acting conductor), and Gareth Williams (early arrangements).

'The Ballad of Solomon Jones' recorded at Stinkpole, Chicago; Cousin It's, Pontypool; and Space Studios, Cardiff: **JON LANGFORD** – guitar and vocals. **GUTO DAFIS** – melodeon and vocals. **JULIAN HAYMAN** – mandolin, ukulele and vocals. **MARK PRICE** – bass. **DEAN CRINDAU** – drumkit. Mixed at North Branch with Ryan Neuschafer.

'Butter Song' originally written for Doorijka Theatre's production of *Bathe Me! – Dr. Faustus Lights the Lights*, adapted from the play by Gertrude Stein.

'Message from Newport' delivered by Johnny Sicolo, Prince of Wales and benevolent Tsar of the legendary TJ's, Clarence Place, Gwent City. Field recording by Carlton B. Morgan.

SKULL ORCHARD REVISITED

Jon Langford with the Burlington Welsh Male Chorus

1   TUBBY BROTHERS
2   VERDUN
3   LAST COUNT
4   BUTTER SONG
5   SENTIMENTAL MARCHING SONG
6   YOUGHAL
7   TRAP DOOR
8   INSIDE THE WHALE
9   I AM THE LAW
10 GREEN VALLEYS
11 PILL SAILOR
12 PENNY ARCADES
13 MY OWN WORST ENEMY
15 I'M STOPPING THIS TRAIN
16 DEEP SEA DIVER
17 TOM JONES LEVITATION
18 THE BALLAD OF SOLOMON JONES
19 MESSAGE FROM NEWPORT

All songs written by Jon Langford. Published by Low Noise Music, Inc.